Goodnight Desd

(Good Morning

D0005641

Ann-Marie MacDonald

Goodnight Desdemona

(Good Morning Juliet)

Coach House Press · Toronto

The punctuation of this play carefully adheres to the
author's instructions. The text combines prose and blank
verse; text in blank verse is indented. Direct quotes from
Shakespeare are set in *Zapf Chancery Italic.*
Thanks to Cheryl, Mo and B.
The Bard is immanent, and beyond thanks.

Published with the assistance of the Canada Council
and the Ontario Arts Council.

FOURTH PRINTING

Printed in Canada

CANADIAN CATALOGUING IN PUBLICATION DATA

MacDonald, Ann-Marie, 1958-
Goodnight Desdemona (Good Morning Juliet)
A play.
ISBN 0-88910-412-3

1. Desdemona (Fictitious character) – Drama.
2. Juliet (Fictitious character) – Drama.
I. Title.

PS8575.D54G66 1990   C812'.54   C90-093660-6
PR9199.3.M336G66 1990

This book is dedicated to you, gentle reader.

'The individual, on his lonely path, needs a secret;
only a secret which he cannot betray – one which
he fears to give away, or which he cannot
formulate into words, and which therefore seems
to belong to the category of crazy ideas – can
prevent the otherwise inevitable retrogression.'
– C.G. JUNG

to go backward esp.
in a worse
condition.

Introduction. ❧

It began with a joke. On a tour of England in 1985 with
This Is For You, Anna, Ann-Marie MacDonald crammed
a pillow on my face and with great hilarity pronounced:
'Goodnight, Desdemona!' Something snapped, a clear
light sound pervaded the air, and a masterpiece was
born. If that is not exactly what happened, it is certainly
true that for the following years the bon mot floated
around as the tip of an iceberg.

Nightwood Theatre accepted the title as a show in
their upcoming season, and it was produced in 1988, on
March 31, at the Annex Theatre in Toronto. The original
cast included Tanja Jacobs as Constance, Derek Boyes as
Othello/Tybalt, Beverley Cooper as Juliet, Diana
Fajrajsl as Desdemona, and Martin Julien as Iago/
Romeo. Skip Shand was my Assistant Director.

Ann-Marie MacDonald and I have had many working relationships since we met in 1983. We have been fellow performers, fellow writers, fellow administrators, I
writer, you actor, I director, you actor, and now here we
had come to I director, you writer. *Goodnight Desdemona* was her first solo flight.

The script we received on the first day of rehearsal was
far more weighty, complex, and erudite than anyone had
expected. We expected plot and wit, yes, but 100 and
some pages, no. The paltry three weeks we had for
rehearsal were a wild scramble to workshop the script
and get it on stage. The dramaturgical abilities of the
entire cast were brought into play, especially the critical
intelligence of Tanja Jacobs, who, after all, faced more
lines than Hamlet.

The success of that first production was due predomi-
nantly to the brio of text and acting. As a director, it is

really only now, more than a year later, that I can relish the play as a theatrical event, while we are conducting rehearsals for the second production. The text has settled down, the characters have been refined, and the play can be explored. With Kate Lynch now in the role of Constance, and Sue LePage as the designer, the process is fresh in more ways than one.

With *Goodnight Desdemona*, Ann-Marie MacDonald has created her own alchemical manuscript. The play proceeds in a hermetic landscape of thought, setting and character, in which even the most unusual events make perfect logical sense. With her own love of whodunit, MacDonald has woven mystery into mystery. The story seems to be a fantasy of a dusty academic, Constance, who falls into two Shakespearean plays, changes the story, meets Desdemona and Juliet, and finds out that she is the author of the tale. This does not mean that Constance is really 'Mrs.' Shakespeare, however. The real story happens in the zone of the unconscious mind. Constance stews in her office like base matter in an alchemical dish; she reaches the nigredo/nadir of her existence, and this allows her to reconsider her life, her self, as if in a dream. Desdemona and Juliet are archetypes of her own unconscious, Othello and Tybalt are permutations of Professor Night, and the Chorus, Iago and Yorick can be seen as versions of her own goading animus. But if we push the alchemical and Jungian concepts aside, the story still stands – perfectly – as a re-visioning of some of Shakespeare's best characters.

Ann-Marie MacDonald was trained as an actor and, after some brushes with establishment theatre, plunged into collective and collaborative ventures. For the director and the ensemble, this experience pays off in the text. There is no one actor who plays merely the spectator or the stooge. Neither is there a star; even though Constance is definitely the lead character, all other parts are equally balanced and work together throughout every scene. There is an abundance of twists, fights, dances, wild surprises, which result in an absolute joy of play. The piece requires a gusto, an energy, top comic skills as well as the ability to translate the internal to the level of the gestural and the mythic.

MacDonald's love of the theatre translates into the production as well. Heads are to come out of wastebaskets, turtles are ripped apart, ghosts walk the earth, and someone magically disappears. These visions are by no means intended as filmic; quite the contrary, they come from an understanding of theatricality as it was practised a century ago. The theatre can conjure anything, MacDonald says, and it doesn't need the cinema to help it along.

For myself, the greatest pleasure of the piece is its scope – in terms of content, in terms of theatricality, and ultimately, in terms of the place it gives women. The women of *Goodnight Desdemona* are always active, always pushing the piece forward, threatening, seducing, giving up, rallying, stabbing, kissing, embracing, thinking. Their astounding variety seems logical considering the woman who created them. After all, Ann-Marie MacDonald is herself a feminist, a raconteur, adventurer, actor and scholar with a Sargasso Sea of a mind.

Baṇuta Rubess
Toronto, December 1989

Goodnight Desdemona (Good Morning Juliet) was commissioned and first produced by Nightwood Theatre in 1988 at Toronto's Annex Theatre with the following company:

Derek Boyes *Othello, Tybalt, Professor Claude Night, Juliet's Nurse*
Beverley Cooper *Juliet, Student, Soldier of Cyprus*
Diana Fajrajsl *Desdemona, Ramona, Mercutio, Servant*
Tanja Jacobs *Constance Ledbelly*
Martin Julien *Romeo, Chorus, Iago, Ghost*

Director and Dramaturge: Baṇuta Rubess
Stage Manager: Maria Popoff
Assistant Director: Skip Shand
Set and Costume Design: Denyse Karn
Prop Design: Joan Parkinson
Lighting: Dorian Clark
Sound and Original Music: Nic Gotham
Fight Director: Robert Lindsay
Choreographer: Susan McKenzie

In a revised text, the play was subsequently toured by Nightwood Theatre in 1990 to Great Canadian Theatre Company, Northern Light Theatre, Vancouver East Cultural Centre, and The Canadian Stage Company, with the following company:

Derek Boyes *Othello, Tybalt, Professsor Claude
    Night, Juliet's Nurse*
Beverley Cooper *Juliet, Student, Soldier of Cyprus*
Diana Fajrajsl *Desdemona, Ramona, Mercutio,
    Servant*
Kate Lynch *Constance Ledbelly*
Martin Julien *Romeo, Chorus, Iago, Ghost*

Director and Dramaturge: Banuta Rubess
Stage Manager: Maria Popoff
Set, Costume and Prop Design: Sue Le Page
Lighting: Leslie Wilkinson
Production Manager: Glenn Davidson
Sound and Original Music: Nic Gotham
Fight Director: R. H. Thomson
Choreographer: Susan McKenzie

Dramatis Personae. ❧

DESDEMONA

OTHELLO

JULIET

ROMEO

CONSTANCE LEDBELLY, an assistant professor
at Queen's University

CHORUS

STUDENT, 'Julie, uh Jill,' a student at Queen's
University

IAGO

RAMONA, a student at Queen's University

TYBALT

MERCUTIO

PROFESSOR CLAUDE NIGHT, a professor at Queen's
University, and boss to Constance Ledbelly

A SOLDIER OF CYPRUS

JULIET'S NURSE

SERVANT

GHOST

Act I, The Dumbshow.

a decorative design at the beginning of a play

Three vignettes played simultaneously.

1 – Desdemona's bedchamber; OTHELLO *murders* DESDEMONA *in her bed, by smothering her with a pillow.*

2 – A crypt; ROMEO *dead,* JULIET *unconscious on a slab.* JULIET *awakens, sees* ROMEO, *and kills herself with his rapier.*

3 – Constance Ledbelly's office at Queen's University; CONSTANCE *finishes a telephone conversation. She is upset. She hangs up the phone, takes her green plumed fountain pen from behind her ear, and pitches it into the wastebasket. She then picks up a long and narrow, ancient leather-bound manuscript, pitches it in after the pen, and exits.*

Act I, The Prologue.

Constance's office at Queen's University, Kingston.
The CHORUS *enters Constance's office by a route that suggests he is not bound by the reality of the office walls. He lights a cigarette and speaks the prologue.*

CHORUS   What's alchemy? The hoax of charlatans?
           Or mystic quest for stuff of life itself:
           eternal search for the Philosopher's Stone,
           where mingling and unmingling opposites,
           transforms base metal into precious gold.
           Hence, scientific metaphor of self:
           divide the mind's opposing archetypes
           – if you possess the courage for the task –
           invite them from the shadows to the light;
           unite these lurking shards of broken glass
           into a mirror that reflects one soul.

And in this merging of unconscious selves,
there lies the mystic 'marriage of true minds.'
[*he takes the discarded objects from the wastebasket and
replaces them on the desk as:*]
Swift Mercury, that changing element,
portrayed as Gemini, hermaphrodite and twin,
now steers the stars of Constance Ledbelly,
and offers her a double-edged re-birthday.
[*he picks up the manuscript from the wastebasket and
replaces it on the desk. An unintelligible inscription on the
cover is now apparent*]
Here is the key to her Philosopher's Stone –
[*indicates manuscript*]
the psychic altar that will alter fate.
But she has not the eyes to see it … yet.
[*The* CHORUS *butts out his cigarette on the floor next to her
desk and exits as:*]

Act I, Scene i. ❧

Constance's office.
CONSTANCE *enters her office, absently humming and occa-
sionally singing, 'Fairy Tales Can Come True.' She wears a
coat, boots, and a bright red woolen toque with a pom-pom
at the end. She is laden with a bookbag, a 'Complete Works
of Shakespeare' and a stack of dog-eared loose-leaf foolscap.
The telephone rings, but* CONSTANCE, *in the middle of jot-
ting down a particularly salient note on her foolscap, only
manages to lay her hand on the phone just as it ceases to ring.
She removes her coat, under which she wears a crumpled
tweedy skirt and jacket suit. She forgets to remove her toque
and wears it throughout the scene. She sits down at her desk,
opens a drawer, and takes out a package of Velveeta cheese*

upon which she nibbles while warming to her subject.
Throughout the rest of the scene CONSTANCE *works aloud
on her doctoral thesis: a copious dog-eared document
handwritten in green ink on foolscap.*

CONSTANCE Pen ...
[*she searches, then finds her pen behind her ear*]
'"Romeo and Juliet" and "Othello": The Seeds of
Corruption and Comedy.' Of all Shakespeare's
tragedies, 'Othello' and 'Romeo and Juliet' produce the
most ambivalent and least Aristotelean responses. In
neither play do the supposedly fate-ordained deaths of
the flawed heroes and heroines, seem quite inevitable.
Indeed, it is only because the deaths do occur that they
can be called inevitable in hindsight, thus allowing the
plays to squeak by under the designation, 'tragedy.' But
this retroactively assigned 'inevitability' is never quite
convincing. Fate seems too generous in both plays. In
both plays, the tragic characters, particularly Romeo and
Othello, have abundant opportunity to save themselves.
The fact that they do not save themselves, tends to
characterize them more as the unwitting victims of a
disastrous practical joke – rather than the heroic
instruments of an inexorable Fate. Insofar as these plays
may be said to be fatalistic at all, any grains of authentic
tragedy must be seen to reside in the heroines,
Desdemona and Juliet.
[*A sheaf of papers slides under the office door.* CONSTANCE
*goes to the door and stoops to pick them up just as they begin
to slide out again. A little tug of war ensues. Suddenly the
door opens against* CONSTANCE*'s head. She stands up to see
a young female* STUDENT]
STUDENT I'm sorry Miss Ledbelly, I thought you were out.
CONSTANCE Oh. Um. I'm in.

[STUDENT *takes the sheaf from* CONSTANCE *and writes on it*]

STUDENT I put the incorrect date on my essay.

CONSTANCE Oh. What's today?

STUDENT It's the first.

CONSTANCE The first what?

STUDENT Of the month.

CONSTANCE Oh.

[STUDENT *hands essay back to* CONSTANCE]

STUDENT I know it's a week past the due date but [*lying*] you remember the extension you gave me, eh?

CONSTANCE I did?

STUDENT Yes, because I've been ill lately. [*cough-cough*]

CONSTANCE Oh yes, well, whatever, that's fine.

STUDENT Thanks Miss Ledbelly.

CONSTANCE Wha – uh, what was this assignment?

STUDENT 'The Effect of Filth on Renaissance Drama.'

CONSTANCE Good. That sounds just fine Julie, uh Jill uh ... keep up the good work.

STUDENT Thanks, Miss. By the way, I like your hair like that. It's really pretty.

CONSTANCE Oh.

[*she vaguely touches her hair below the toque*]
Thanks.

[*Exit* STUDENT. CONSTANCE *closes the door then, stuffing the student's essay into her bookbag*]
Lie thou there. Now where was I?

[*she takes a bite of Velveeta and settles down to work*]
Uh, At ... At the tragic turning point in 'Othello' even the hardened fatalist is at pains to suppress a cry of warning, *id est,* 'O Othello, O Tragic Man, stop your ears against the false yapping of that cur, Iago. The divine Desdemona, despite her fascination with violence and her love of horror stories, and aside from

the fact that she deceived her father to elope with you, is
the very embodiment of purity and charity.'
[CONSTANCE *opens her Shakespeare, oblivious to*
OTHELLO *and* IAGO *who enter and play out the following
scene which she reads silently to herself*]

IAGO My Lord Othello, *Did Cassio, when you wooed
Desdemona, know of your love?*

OTHELLO *He did from first to last,* Iago.
And went between us very oft.

IAGO *Indeed?*

OTHELLO *Indeed? Ay, indeed! Discern'st thou aught in that?
Is he not honest?*

IAGO *Honest, my lord?*

OTHELLO *Honest? Ay,
honest.*

IAGO *My lord, for aught I know.*

OTHELLO *What dost thou think?*

IAGO *Think, my lord?*

OTHELLO *Think, my
lord?
By heaven thou echoest me,
as if there were some monster in thy thought
too hideous to be shown. Thou dost mean something.
If thou dost love me, show me thy thought.*

IAGO *My lord, you know I love you.*

[CONSTANCE *takes a previously opened can of Coors Light
beer from her desk drawer and sips it*]

CONSTANCE We are willing to accept Iago's effortless seduction of
Othello unto foaming jealousy – the Moor is, after all, an
aging warrior, in love with honour and young
Desdemona –

[CONSTANCE *turns a page of Shakespeare. Back to*
OTHELLO *and* IAGO]

OTHELLO *Villain, be sure thou prove my love a whore!*

Be sure of it; give me the ocular proof.

IAGO *Tell me but this:*
Have you not sometimes seen a handkerchief
spotted with strawberries in your wife's hand?

OTHELLO *I gave her such a one; 'twas my first gift.*

IAGO *I know not that; but such a handkerchief —*
I am sure it was your wife's — did I today
see Cassio wipe his beard with.

OTHELLO *If it be that —*

IAGO *If it be that, or any that was hers,*
It speaks against her with the other proofs.

OTHELLO *Had Desdemona forty thousand lives!*
One is too poor, too weak for my revenge.
Damn her, lewd minx! O, damn her! Damn her! O!
I will chop her into messes! Cuckold me!

IAGO *O, 'tis foul in her.*

OTHELLO *With mine officer!*

IAGO *That's fouler.*

OTHELLO *Get me some poison, Iago, this night.*

IAGO *Do it not with poison. Strangle her in bed, even the bed*
she hath contaminated.

OTHELLO *Good, good! The justice of it pleases. Very good! Now art*
thou my lieutenant.

IAGO *I am your own forever.*

[OTHELLO *and* IAGO *embrace, then exit*]

CONSTANCE — but we cannot help suspect that all might still so easily
be set to rights; and *there's the rub!* For it is this suspicion
which corrupts our pure experience of fear and pity at a
great man's great plight, and — by the end of the
handkerchief scene — threatens to leave us, frankly …
irritated.

[CONSTANCE *sips her beer just as the door bursts open.*
Another young female student, RAMONA, *stands in the*
doorway, all business and very assertive]

RAMONA Hello Professor, my name is Ramona.

CONSTANCE I'm not actually – I'm, I'm just an Assistant Professor.

[CONSTANCE *suddenly remembers her beer, and conceals it*]

RAMONA Oh. Well, I wonder if you could pass on a message to Claude for me.

CONSTANCE Claude? Oh, you mean Professor Night?

RAMONA Yes. Just tell him I won the Rhodes.

CONSTANCE Congratulations ... Ramona.

RAMONA Thanks. By the way, Coors beer supports the Contras.

CONSTANCE Oh. Sorry. It ... was a gift.

[*Exit* RAMONA. CONSTANCE *picks up her beer, goes to throw it away, looks around, then drains it furtively and pitches it into the wastebasket*]

In 'Romeo and Juliet,' Shakespeare sets the stage for comedy with the invocation of those familiar comic themes, love-at-first-sight, and the fickleness of youth. But no sooner has our appetite for comedy been whetted, when Tybalt slays Mercutio, and poor Romeo proceeds to leave a trail of bodies in his wake.

[CONSTANCE *turns another page of her Shakespeare. Enter* TYBALT *and* MERCUTIO]

TYBALT *Mercutio, thou consortest with Romeo.*

MERCUTIO *Consort? What Tybalt, dost thou make us minstrels? And thou make minstrels of us, look to hear nothing but discords. Here's my fiddlestick;* [*indicates sword*] *here's that shall make you dance.*

[*Enter* ROMEO]

TYBALT *Romeo, the love I bear thee can afford*
no better term than this: thou art a villain.

ROMEO *Tybalt, the reason that I have to love thee*
doth much excuse the appertaining rage
to such a greeting. Villain am I none.
Therefore farewell. I see thou knowest me not.

TYBALT   *Boy, this shall not excuse the injuries*
that thou hast done me; therefore turn and draw.

ROMEO   *I do protest I never injured thee,*
But love thee better than thou canst devise
till thou shalt know the reason of my love;
And so, good Capulet, which name I tender
as dearly as mine own, be satisfied.

MERCUTIO   *O calm, dishonorable, vile submission!*
[draws] Tybalt, you ratcatcher, will you walk?

CONSTANCE   If only Romeo would confess to Tybalt that he has just
become his cousin-in-law by marrying Juliet. Such is our
corrupt response that begs the question, 'Is this
tragedy?!' Or is it comedy gone awry, when a host of
comic devices is pressed into the blood-soaked service of
tragic ends?

TYBALT   *[draws] I am for you.*

ROMEO   *Gentle Mercutio, put thy rapier up.*

MERCUTIO   *Come sir, your passado!*
*[*TYBALT *and* MERCUTIO *fight]*

ROMEO   *Hold Tybalt! Good Mercutio!*
*[*TYBALT, *under* ROMEO's *arm, thrusts* MERCUTIO *in,*
and flies]
Courage, man. The hurt cannot be much.

MERCUTIO   *Why the devil came you between us? I was hurt under*
your arm. A plague a both your houses!
*[*MERCUTIO *exits and dies. Enter* TYBALT *]*

ROMEO   *Alive in triumph, and Mercutio slain? [he draws]*

TYBALT   *Thou wretched boy that didst consort him here,*
shalt with him hence.
[They fight. TYBALT *falls]*

ROMEO   *O, I am fortune's fool!*
[Exit ROMEO, TYBALT, MERCUTIO. CONSTANCE
reaches into her bookbag and withdraws a pack of Player's
Extra Light cigarettes. It's empty. She spots the Chorus's

cigarette butt on the floor, picks it up and carefully begins to repair it]

CONSTANCE What if a Fool were to enter the worlds of both 'Othello' and 'Romeo and Juliet'? Would he be akin to the Wise Fool in 'King Lear'?: a Fool who can comfort and comment, but who cannot alter the fate of the tragic hero. Or would our Fool defuse the tragedies by assuming centre stage as comic hero? Indeed, in 'Othello' and 'Romeo and Juliet' the Fool is conspicuous by his very absence, for these two tragedies turn on flimsy mistakes – a lost hanky, a delayed wedding announcement – mistakes too easily concocted and corrected by a Wise Fool. I will go further: are these mistakes, in fact, the footprints of a missing Fool?; a Wise Fool whom Shakespeare eliminated from two earlier comedies by an unknown author?! *Non obstante*; although a Fool might stem the blundering of Othello and Romeo, the question remains, would he prove a match ... [*she pops the cigarette butt between her lips and hunts for a match*] for Desdemona and Juliet? Is there any Fool equal to the task of wrenching comedy forth their fatal hearts? Or are these excellent heroines fated to remain tragedies looking for a place to happen? [*having failed to find a match, she tosses the cigarette butt into the wastebasket, then opens the ancient Manuscript. It is the same length and width as foolscap. She becomes momentarily absorbed in it, trying to decipher it, turning it every which way*] Nevertheless. I postulate that the Gustav Manuscript, when finally decoded, will prove the prior existence of two comedies by an unknown author; comedies that Shakespeare plundered and made over into ersatz tragedies! It is an irresistible – if wholly repugnant – thought.

[*The office door begins to open silently. Oblivious,*

CONSTANCE *resumes her soft tuneless singing. She takes up her fountain pen once more but discovers it is out of ink. She bends down to her bookbag on the floor to look for a refill and does not see* PROFESSOR CLAUDE NIGHT *enter on tip-toe. He is about the same age as Constance, is perfectly groomed and brogued, speaks with an Oxford accent, and oozes confidence. He silently perches on her desk. She rises from the depths of her bookbag, sees him, and hits the roof*] Ah-h-h!

PROFESSOR   Heh-heh-heh, got you again Connie.

CONSTANCE   Heh. Oh Professor Night, you scared the daylights out of me.

PROFESSOR   You must learn to relax, my little titmouse. You're working too hard. Speaking of which … have you got something for me? [CONSTANCE *stares at him for a moment too long before answering*]

CONSTANCE   Yes. It's here somewhere.

[*She begins rummaging.* PROFESSOR *picks up her green-ink thesis. He shakes his head.* CONSTANCE *surfaces from her desk with a thick essay, also handwritten in green ink on foolscap. She sees that he is reading her thesis. She shoots out her hand involuntarily and snatches it from him*]
Don't read that! … sir … the ink's not dry.
[*She stuffs her thesis into a drawer of her desk. He wipes his green ink-stained fingers on his handkerchief*]

PROFESSOR   Still harping on the Gustav Manuscript are you? I hate to see you turning into a laughing stock Connie. You know you'll never get your doctorate at this rate.

CONSTANCE   I know … I guess I just have a thing for lost causes.

PROFESSOR   You're an incurable romantic Connie.

CONSTANCE   Just a failed existentialist.

PROFESSOR   Traipsing after the Holy Grail, or the Golden Fleece or some such figment.

CONSTANCE   It could be the Missing Link in Shakespeare.

PROFESSOR   It could be a joke. No one takes it seriously anymore.

CONSTANCE Whoever cracks the Gustav code will be right up there
with Darwin, Bingham –

PROFESSOR And Don Quixote. The best tenured minds in the world
have sought to translate it for the past three hundred
years. What gives you the notion you're special?

CONSTANCE Oh I'm not, I'm, I'm not the least bit special, I'm, I'm just
one flawed and isolated fragment of a perfect infinite
mind like anybody else, I – I think that I exist in that you
and I are here chatting with the sense evidence of each
other, insofar as we're not over there not chatting, no I'm
not special – unique maybe, in the, in the sense that a
snowflake is unique, but no more valuable than any
other flake ... It's just that I, I did win the Dead
Languages Prize as an undergraduate, and it would be a
shame to hide my light under a bushel.

PROFESSOR [*concealing his curiosity*] Say you did crack these obscure
alchemical hieroglyphs; what if they turned out to be a
grocery list or some such rubbish?

CONSTANCE Well I, I just have this indefensible thesis that it's
something important.

PROFESSOR Such as?

CONSTANCE I think it's source material that Shakespeare wanted to
suppress yet preserve.

PROFESSOR But Shakespeare's sources are no secret.

CONSTANCE This one is. This one could undermine two of
Shakespeare's foremost tragedies. It's by an unknown
author –

PROFESSOR And I suppose you've feverishly identified a whole raft of
anagrams to support this heresy?

CONSTANCE As a matter of fact, yes. If you take the second letter of
the eighteenth word of every second scene in 'Othello,'
and cross reference them with the corresponding letters
in 'Romeo and Juliet,' it says: 'I dare not name the source
of this txt.'

PROFESSOR 'txt'?

CONSTANCE Well, 'text.' I'm missing the letter, 'e,' it was probably deleted in a later printing.

PROFESSOR Your fascination with mystery borders on the vulgar, I'm afraid.

CONSTANCE I can't help it. I'm a fallen Catholic. It's left me with a streak of 'whodunit.'

PROFESSOR Well who did dun it? What became of this mysterious source material?

CONSTANCE I think Shakespeare gave it to his elderly friend, Gustav the alchemist, to shroud in an arcane code, and that's what's in here.

PROFESSOR [*amused*] Oh Connie. You have such an interesting little mind.

CONSTANCE Thank you sir.

PROFESSOR Hand it over.

[CONSTANCE *thinks he is referring to the Manuscript*]

No, ye gods forfend, not that decrepit tome. The – ahem – your latest commission.

CONSTANCE Oh, the essay. Here you go. I hope I've destroyed Professor Hollowfern's book to your satisfaction.

PROFESSOR I'm sure its up to your customarily dizzying standard. Did you remember to give yourself the usual thanks for 'irksome proofing of the text'?

CONSTANCE [*beet red*] In point of fact sir, I took the liberty of dedicating it to myself.

PROFESSOR That's awfully sweet of you Connie. [*looks at essay*] Tsk tsk tsk your hand gets more cryptic all the time. Like the tracks of some tiny green creature. I do wish you'd learn to type, my dear. I'm weary of doing my own typing, and I daren't trust anyone else with our little secret.

CONSTANCE I'm working on it sir, but my fine motor skills are really poor.

PROFESSOR [*still scanning the essay*] Indeed.

CONSTANCE I'm ready for my next assignment Professor. I've sharpened my nib to a killing point.
[*They share a malicious chuckle*]

PROFESSOR And dipped it in venom to paralyze the academic foe with one poisonous phrase?
[*more chuckling*]

CONSTANCE Just name your victim.

PROFESSOR Connie. There remains but one thing you can do for me.

CONSTANCE Oh? ... What's that?
[*He takes a small velvet box from his pocket, opens it and shows her*]

PROFESSOR Tell me ... do you like it?

CONSTANCE Oh Professor Night –

PROFESSOR Claude.

CONSTANCE Oh Claude ... it's the most beautiful diamond I've ever seen.

PROFESSOR Dear Connie. Thank you. I'm the happiest man in the world.

CONSTANCE So am I. I can't quite believe it!

PROFESSOR Neither will Ramona.

CONSTANCE Ramona? ... Oh.

PROFESSOR I'm going to miss you Connie.

CONSTANCE Am I going somewhere?

PROFESSOR I am, pet. I've decided to take that lecturing post at Oxford myself. Even if it does fall somewhat short of a challenge.

CONSTANCE Oh. I thought you might recommend someone less distinguished, say an Assistant Professor, for that job.

PROFESSOR That's what I thought too until Ramona won the Rhodes. Now it's Oxford for the both of us, eh what?

CONSTANCE What about – Will I still work for you?

PROFESSOR I'm afraid not love. I made full Professor today, so the pressure's off.

CONSTANCE Congratulations.

PROFESSOR   Not to worry. I've lined up a lovely post for you in
             Regina.
CONSTANCE   Thanks.
PROFESSOR   What's your schedule like day after tomorrow? I hoped
             you'd help pack my books.
CONSTANCE   I'd love to but ... that's my birthday ... and I planned on
             going to the zoo.
PROFESSOR   Birthday eh? Chalk up another one for the Grim Reaper.
             Still twenty-nine and holding are we? Well, many happy
             re-runs. [*chuckle*] I've got to dash. I'm addressing the
             Literary Society this evening – which reminds me!
             [*But* CONSTANCE *has anticipated him, and hands him
             another sheaf of inky green foolscap*]
CONSTANCE   Here's your speech.
PROFESSOR   Thanks old girl.
             [*He tugs the pom-pom on her toque then exits with:*]
             Oxford ho!
             [CONSTANCE *slowly pulls off her toque and drops it into the
             wastebasket. She is in shock. This is the nadir of her passage
             on this earth*]
CONSTANCE   Regina. I hate the prairies. They're flat. It's an absolute
             nightmare landscape of absolutes and I'm a relativist, I'll
             go mad. Diamonds are a girl's best friend. Diamonds are
             harder than a bed of nails. I can't feel anything. I'm
             perfectly fine. I'll call the Dean and resign. I'll go back to
             my apartment and watch the plants die and let the cats
             copulate freely. I'll order in groceries. Eventually I'll be
             evicted. I'll smell really bad and swear at people on the
             subway. Five years later I run into Professor Night and
             Ramona: they don't recognize me. I'm selling pencils.
             They buy one. Suddenly, I drop dead. They discover my
             true identity. I'm awarded my doctorate posthumously.
             Professor Night dedicates his complete works to me and
             lays roses on my grave every day. My stone bears a simple

epithet: 'Oh what a noble mind is here o'erthrown.' ...
There's no time to lose! I have to start right now if I'm
going to sink that low in five years. [*grabs phone, dials*]
Hello, give me the office of the Dean! ... Oh yes, I'll
hold. [*while holding, she surveys the objects on her desk,
picks them up one by one, addresses them, then tosses them
into the wastebasket*] The bronze wings that my Brownie
pack gave me. [*reads inscription*] 'To the best Brown Owl
in the forest.' I flew up more girls than any Brown Owl
other than Lady Baden Powell. [*toss. Picks up a jar that
contains something like an anchovy*] My appendix. It was
removed in the summer of love when the rest of my
family went to Expo '67. The doctor gave it to me in this
baby food jar. He thought it would cheer me up. It did.
[*toss. Takes the plumed fountain pen from behind her ear*]
The fountain pen I made from my parakeet, Laurel. She
used to sing 'Volare.' She fell five stories and died
instantly. [*goes to toss it away, but cannot bear to do so. She
replaces it behind her ear, where it stays for the rest of the
play. Picks up the Manuscript*] And this – my fool's gold.
Silent mocking oracle. I'll do the world a favour.

[CONSTANCE *goes to toss it in the wastebasket but her
gesture is suddenly arrested in midair and she stares,
spellbound, at the inscription on the cover. Harp music and
light effects. She blinks and tries to focus, as though the
inscription were swimming before her eyes with a
disorienting effect.* CONSTANCE *reads the inscription
aloud:*]

'You who possess the eyes to see
this strange and wondrous alchemy,
where words transform to vision'ry,
where one plus two makes one, not three;
open this book if you agree
to be illusion's refugee,

and of return no guarantee –
unless you find your true identity.
And discover who the Author be.'
[CONSTANCE *hesitates for a moment, then opens the Manuscript. Its three pages fall out and down into the wastebasket.* CONSTANCE *sets the cover on her desk, then stoops and reaches into the wastebasket to retrieve the pages. Suddenly her arm jerks downward; she is being pulled down into the wastebasket. 'Warp' effects, sound of screeching wind and music.*
When the sound and lights return to normal in Constance's office, she is nowhere to be seen. The phone receiver dangles off the hook. Smoke issues from the wastebasket. The CHORUS*'s head, a cigarette between his lips, emerges from the wastebasket*]

CHORUS   You've witnessed an impossible event:
a teacher, spinster – 'old maid,' some would say –
whose definition of fun and excitement
is a run of 'ibids' in an essay,
disappears before your very eyes.
Suspend your disbelief. Be foolish wise.
For anything is possible, you'll find,
within the zone of the unconscious mind.
[*His head disappears back into the wastebasket. During the scene-change, we hear* OTHELLO *and* IAGO *via their enhanced voice-over:*]

IAGO   *Think, my lord?*
OTHELLO   *Think, my lord? By heaven he echoes me.*
IAGO   *Indeed?*
OTHELLO   *Indeed? Ay indeed!*
IAGO   *Think, my lord?*
OTHELLO   *Think, my lord? Ay!*
IAGO   *Have you not sometimes seen a handkerchief?*
OTHELLO   *If it be that –*

IAGO   *If it be that —*
OTHELLO   *Goats and Monkeys!*
IAGO   *Indeed.*

Act II, Scene i. ✿

Othello's citadel at Cyprus.
OTHELLO *and* IAGO *reprise the end of the 'Handkerchief Scene.' Desdemona's 'strawberry-spotted' handkerchief hangs out the back of* IAGO*'s hose.*

IAGO   *Tell me but this:*
            Have you not sometimes seen a handkerchief
            spotted with strawberries in your wife's hand?
OTHELLO   *I gave her such a one; 'twas my first gift.*
IAGO   *I know not that; but such a handkerchief —*
            I am sure it was your wife's — did I today
            see Cassio wipe his beard with.
OTHELLO   *If it be that —*
IAGO   *If it be that, or any that was hers,*
            It speaks against her with the other proofs.
            [CONSTANCE*'s head peeks out from behind an arras*]
OTHELLO   *Had Desdemona forty thousand lives!*
            One is too poor, too weak for my revenge.
            Damn her, lewd minx! O, damn her! Damn her, O!
            I will chop her into messes! Cuckold me!
IAGO   *O, 'tis foul in her.*
OTHELLO   *With mine officer!*
IAGO   *That's fouler.*
OTHELLO   *Get me some poison Iago, this night.*
IAGO   *Do it not with poison.*
            [IAGO *hands a pillow to* OTHELLO]
            Strangle her in bed.

CONSTANCE No!

[*Both* OTHELLO *and* IAGO *turn and stare at her, amazed*]

Um ... you're about to make a terrible mistake ... m'Lord.

[*Shocked, and at a loss for words to explain her statement,* CONSTANCE *gathers her courage and timidly approaches* IAGO]

Excuse me please.

[*She plucks the handkerchief from* IAGO*'s hose and gives it to* OTHELLO]

OTHELLO Desdemona's handkerchief! [*to* IAGO] Which thou didst say she gave to Cassio!

IAGO Did I say that? What I meant to say –

OTHELLO O-o-o! *I see that nose of thine, but not that dog I shall throw it to!*

IAGO My lord, I can explain –

CONSTANCE Omigod, what have I done?

[*She grabs the handkerchief from* OTHELLO *and tries unsuccessfully to stuff it back into* IAGO*'s pocket*]

Look, just forget you ever saw me here, okay?!

[*She grabs the pillow and offers it to* OTHELLO]

Here.

[OTHELLO *ignores the pillow and proceeds to bind and threaten* IAGO]

  [*aside*] I've wrecked a masterpiece. I've ruined the
    play,
  I've turned Shakespeare's 'Othello' to a farce.
  O Jesus, they've got swords! And this is Cyprus;
  there's a war on here! O please wake up.
  Please be a dream. I've got to get back home!
  Back to my cats. They'll starve. They'll eat the
    plants.
  They'll be so lonely. [*to* OTHELLO] Please! I've got to
    go!

	Where's the exit!?
OTHELLO	Stay!!!
CONSTANCE	Sure.
OTHELLO	Forty-thousand lives were not enough
	to satisfy my debt to you, strange friend.
	I'd keep you on this island till I knew
	which angel beached you on our war-like shores,
	and how you gained fair knowledge of foul deeds.
CONSTANCE	Well. Actually. I've studied you for years.
OTHELLO	You must be a learn'ed oracle.
	I'd have you nightly search the firmament,
	and daily read the guts of sheep for signs
	to prophesy our battles with the Turk.
CONSTANCE	I only know of your domestic life.
OTHELLO	And of the murd'rous viper in my breast.
	My shame is deeper than the Pontic sea,
	which yet would drown in my remorseful tears,
	whose crashing waves are mute before the trumpet cry
	of this atoning heart would tumble Jericho!
CONSTANCE	Oh well, I wouldn't dwell on it too much.
	You'd never have been jealous on your own.
OTHELLO	O yes, I had forgot. [*to* IAGO] 'Twas all thy fault.
	[*to* CONSTANCE] If that you be the mirror of my soul,
	then you must learn the story of my life:
	of moving accidents by flood and field,
	of hairbreadth scapes i' th' imminent deadly breach,
	of being taken by the insolent foe —
CONSTANCE	Oh yes, I know.
IAGO	[*aside*] So know we all the wag and swagger of this tale.
OTHELLO	In Egypt, kicked I sand into the eyes
	of infidels who thought I made a truce

when I did give to them a pyramid
on wheels they pulled into the garrison.
But I had packed it full with Christian men,
who slit the savage throat of every Turk.

CONSTANCE   That sounds like Troy.

IAGO   [*aside*] Not Troy, but false.

CONSTANCE   And Desdemona fell in love with you,
because she loved to hear you talk of war.

OTHELLO   *These things to hear she seriously inclined.*

CONSTANCE   I've always thought she had a violent streak,
and that she lived vicariously through you,
but no one else sees eye to eye with me.
Yet I maintain, she did elope with you,
and sailed across a war zone just to live
in this armed camp, therefore – [*aside*] He's not a
Moor.

IAGO   [*aside*] Amour? Ah-ha! C'est ça! Et pourquoi pas?!
[*A flourish of martial music*]

OTHELLO   *Here comes the lady. Let her witness it.*
[*Enter* DESDEMONA *attended by a* SOLDIER *who carries
her needlework*]

DESDEMONA   O valiant general and most bloody lord!

OTHELLO   *O my fair warrior!*

DESDEMONA   *My dear Othello!*

CONSTANCE   *Divine Desdemona!*

OTHELLO   My better self!
[OTHELLO *and* DESDEMONA *embrace*]

IAGO   [*aside*] And my escap'ed prey. I'll trap thee yet.

DESDEMONA   *That I love my lord to live with him,
my downright violence and storm of fortunes
may trumpet to the world.* My sole regret –
that heaven had not made me such a man;
but next in honour is to be his wife.
And I love honour more than life! Who's this?

[*Everyone turns and stares at* CONSTANCE]

CONSTANCE Hi ... Desdemona? ... This is like a dream ...
You're just as I imagined you to be.

[CONSTANCE, *in awe, reaches out to touch the hem of* DES-
DEMONA *'s sleeve and fingers it throughout her next speech*]

CONSTANCE I'm Constance Ledbelly. I'm an academic.
I come from Queen's. You're real. You're really real.

DESDEMONA As real as thou art, Constance, Queen of Academe.

CONSTANCE Is that my true identity? Gosh.
I was just a teacher 'til today.

DESDEMONA A learned lady? O most rare in kind.
And does your husband not misprize this
knowledge?

CONSTANCE Oh I'm not married.

IAGO [*aside*] Most unnatural!

OTHELLO A virgin oracle! Thanks be to Dian!

DESDEMONA Brave ag'ed maid, to wander all alone!

CONSTANCE I'm really more of an armchair traveller.
In fact this is the biggest trip I've made.
I've only ever gone on package tours.

DESDEMONA I long to hear the story of your life.

CONSTANCE There isn't much to tell. It's very dull.
I'm certain your life's much much more exciting.

DESDEMONA This modesty becomes your royal self.
Othello, may she lodge with us awhile?

OTHELLO I would she'd never leave these bristling banks.
She hath uncanny knowledge of our lives,
and sees us better than we see ourselves.
[*to* CONSTANCE] So now art thou my oracle and
chaste.

[OTHELLO *grips* CONSTANCE *in a bear hug*]
[*to* DESDEMONA] Hither sent by fortune, she hath
saved me
from *perdition such as nothing else could match.*

Make her a darling like your precious eye.
[*aside to* CONSTANCE] You are her greatest friend.
   But don't tell why.
[*aside to* IAGO] Deliver up the handkerchief, thou
   cur.
[OTHELLO *takes the handkerchief and presents it to* DES-
DEMONA]

IAGO [*aside to* OTHELLO] I was just testing you my lord.
[*Exit* OTHELLO *and* IAGO]

DESDEMONA *If I do vow a friendship, I'll perform it*
to the last article. Othello's honour is my own.
If you do find me foul in this,
then let thy sentence fall upon my life;
as I am brave Othello's faithful wife.
[DESDEMONA *seizes* CONSTANCE *and squeezes her in a*
soldierly embrace]

CONSTANCE Thanks.
[*A blast of trumpets*]
Ah-h!

DESDEMONA Ah, supper. They have killed a suckling pig
in honour of thee.

CONSTANCE   I'm a vegetarian.
That is – I don't eat … flesh. Of any kind.

DESDEMONA Such abstinence is meet in vestal vows,
therefore in all points do I find thee true.
I'd serve thee, Pedant! Beg of me a boon!
Though it be *full of poise and difficult weight,*
and fearful to be granted, I'll perform it!

CONSTANCE There is a problem you could help me with.
I'm not sure how to say this.

DESDEMONA   Speak it plain.

CONSTANCE Alright, I will. I'm from another world –

DESDEMONA Ay, Academe. And ruled by mighty Queens,
a race of Amazons who brook no men.

CONSTANCE	It's really more like –
DESDEMONA	Nothing if not war-like!
	I'd join these ranks of spiked and fighting shes:
	to camp upon the deserts vast and sing
	our songs of conquest, and a dirge or two
	for sisters slain on honour's gory field.
CONSTANCE	If only I could bring you home with me.
DESDEMONA	I'll anywhere with thee, my friend.
CONSTANCE	That's it,
	you see, I can't return until – That is …
	my Queens have charged me with a fearful task:
	I must find out my true identity,
	and then discover who the author be.
DESDEMONA	Thou dost not know thyself?
CONSTANCE	Apparently not.
DESDEMONA	Do none in Academe know who thou art?
CONSTANCE	Maybe. They call me Connie to my face,
	and something else behind my back.
DESDEMONA	What's that?
CONSTANCE	'The Mouse.'
DESDEMONA	'The Mouse'?
CONSTANCE	I saw it carved into a lecture stand.
DESDEMONA	The sculptor dies.
CONSTANCE	Ironic really, since in my world,
	women are supposed to be afraid of mice.
DESDEMONA	O fie, that's base! Where be the Amazons?
CONSTANCE	In fact they're few and far between
	and often shoved to th' fringe.
DESDEMONA	Let's fly to their beleaguered side.
CONSTANCE	My tasks.
DESDEMONA	The first task is performed already Con,
	thou art an Amazon.
CONSTANCE	I'm not so sure.
DESDEMONA	As to the second task, the Author find.

There be no authors here, but warriors.

CONSTANCE   I'm looking for the Author of it all.
How can I put this? Who made you?

DESDEMONA   God made me.

CONSTANCE   But do you know another name for God?

DESDEMONA   God's secret name?

CONSTANCE   That's it! God's secret name.

DESDEMONA   Seek not to know what God would keep a mystery.

CONSTANCE   Have you known God to be called Shakespeare?

DESDEMONA   Shake
Spear? He might be a pagan god of war.

CONSTANCE   This isn't Shakespeare. It must be a source.
Then I was right about the Manuscript!

DESDEMONA   Manuscript?

CONSTANCE   The book that conjured ... this.
It's written by that secret name of God.
If I could find those foolscap pages –

DESDEMONA   Fool's cap?

CONSTANCE   About yea long, and written in a code;
they fell into the garbage. So did I.

DESDEMONA   This Garbage, be it ocean, lake or sea?

CONSTANCE   ... A sea then – if you like – Sargasso Sea.

DESDEMONA   I'll call this quest mine own, my constant friend.
Though I should drown in deep Sargasso Sea,
I'll find thine unknown Author and Fool's Cap,
*for I do love thee! And when I love thee not,
chaos is come again.*
[*A cannon blast.* CONSTANCE *is badly startled. Battle cries
within*]
                        The infidel!
This volley heralds battle with the Turk.
Let's to the sea wall and enjoy the fray!

CONSTANCE   Oh no, I can't. I can't stand violence.

DESDEMONA   If thou wouldst know thyself an Amazon,

acquire a taste for blood. I'll help thee. Come.
[*She takes* CONSTANCE'*s hand and starts to lead her off.*
CONSTANCE *pulls back*]

CONSTANCE No, please!!! I won't look. I'll be sick. I can't even kill a
mosquito!

DESDEMONA Thou shalt be et alive in Cyprus, Con.
Learn to kill.

CONSTANCE No!

DESDEMONA *That's a fault!* Thy sole deficiency.
An errant woman that would live alone,
no husband there, her honour to defend,
must study to be bloody and betimes.

CONSTANCE Please promise me you'll follow your advice.

DESDEMONA So will we both. And we be women; not mice.
Come go with me.

CONSTANCE   Okay, I'll be right there.
[DESDEMONA *exits*]
They can't use real blood, can they?
[*Another cannon blast*]
                              Omigod!
Oh Constance, don't be scared, it's just a play,
and Desdemona will look after you.
Desdemona! I am verging on
the greatest academic breakthrough of
the twentieth century!
I merely must determine authorship.
But have I permanently changed the text?
– You're floundering in the waters of a flood;
the Mona Lisa and a babe float by.
Which one of these two treasures do you save?
I've saved the baby, and let the Mona drown –
Or did the Author know that I'd be coming here,
and leave a part for me to play? How am I cast?
As cast-away to start, but what's my role?

I entered, deus ex machina,
and Desdemona will not die,
because I dropped in from the sky ...
Does that make this a comedy?
And does it prove my thesis true?
In that case, I've preempted the Wise Fool!
He must be here somewhere – I'll track him down
and reinstate him in the text,
and then I'll know who wrote this travesty,
since every scholar worth her salt agrees,
the Fool, is the mouthpiece of the Author!
It's all so strange ... What's even stranger though –
[*she counts the beats of her speech by tapping each of the five fingers of one hand onto the palm of the other, in time with her words*]
I speak in blank verse like the characters:
unrhymed iambical pentameter.
It seems to come quite nat'rally to me.
I feel so eloquent and ... [*making up the missing beats*] eloquent.
My god. Perhaps I'm on an acid trip.
What if some heartless student spiked my beer?!
[*stops counting*] Nonsense. This is my head, this is my pen, this is 'Othello,' Act III Scene iii.
[*Sounds of the fray within*]

DESDEMONA   [*within*] Constance, the fray!
CONSTANCE   Desdemon, I obey!
[CONSTANCE *dashes off toward* DESDEMONA'*s voice*]

Act II, Scene ii. ❦

Same.
Enter IAGO *bearing two buckets of filth on a yoke.*

IAGO   Othello seeks to hide the grisly news
that he did almost kill his guiltless wife,
so dares not gut me openly in law,
but decorates my service with a mean and stinking
yoke. For this, I thank the pedant:
Othello's vestal mascot, Desdemona's cherished pet.
[*takes a Manuscript page from his shirt*]
My wife found this by chance.
It's in no Christian hand, but pigeon pecks –
the script of infidels! Or mayhap not.
Whate'er it be, I will endow it ill,
for it must dovetail with my plot. Let's see:
To 'venge myself upon the bookish mouse,
regain my former credit with my lord,
and undo Desdemona once again ...
How? How? Ah-ha! Confide myself
betrayed by pedant's lies, to Desdemona!;
for she *is of a free and noble nature*
that thinks men honest that but seem to be.
I'll tell her Constance is a spy and whore
would skewer state and marriage on the same cabob!
Thus I blind and train my falcon for the job.
[*Sounds of the battle off, as* CONSTANCE *enters. She does*
not look well. IAGO *withdraws to the shadows, unseen.*
CONSTANCE *collapses on a rampart and hangs her head*
between her knees. DESDEMONA *enters with a severed*
head. Between the lips of the head is a scroll]

DESDEMONA   Constance! Sister! Here's thy boon!
Behold what I have pluck'ed off the beach!
[CONSTANCE *beholds the head and nearly vomits*]
'Tis like to be thy fool's cap. Take it. Read.
[CONSTANCE, *trying not to make eye-contact with the*
head, plucks the scroll from between its teeth. She opens it. A
bowel falls out. She forces herself to read the scroll]

CONSTANCE   Hm ... it's in Sumerian ...

DESDEMONA   Script of infidels!

CONSTANCE   [*reads*] 'The tapestries and portraits of the main hall.
Five spring lambs, all the horse and woman-flesh ...'
This isn't it. This is a looting list.

DESDEMONA   [*addressing head*] Villain! [*tosses head off*]
[CONSTANCE *is about to faint*]
Faint not my noble heart of Academe.
Envision thy worst foe with open gorge.

CONSTANCE   But I don't have a foe.

DESDEMONA   Fie, thou must have!

CONSTANCE   There's only one on earth whom I resent.
But never did he mean to hurt me.

DESDEMONA   Nay?
Who be this false foe?

CONSTANCE   He's Professor Claude Night.

DESDEMONA   What harm to thee?

CONSTANCE   I used to work for him.
For ten years I ... assisted him, by writing.
Some articles he would have writ himself,
had he the time, but he's a busy man.
Now he's got tenure and an Oxford post
I hoped was meant for me.

DESDEMONA   Ten years of ghostly writing for a thief?
Thy mind hath proved a cornucopia
to slake the glutton, sloth, and he hath cooked
his stolen feast on thy Promethean heat.

CONSTANCE   You really think so?

DESDEMONA   Ay! Thou wast in thrall;
ten years an inky slave in paper chains!

CONSTANCE   Yeah.

DESDEMONA   He wears the laurel wreath that should be thine.

CONSTANCE   I guess he does.

DESDEMONA   And commands the legion Academe

	from Lecture Stands that he usurped from thee.
CONSTANCE	What can you do?
DESDEMONA	Gird thou thy trembling loins,
	and slay Professor Night!
CONSTANCE	I'm guilty too:
	I helped him in deceiving Queen's for years.
IAGO	[*aside*] This will serve my turn upon the pedant.
	[*Exit* IAGO]
DESDEMONA	Thine eyes were shrouded by the demon Night,
	and so art thou *more sinned against than sinning.*
CONSTANCE	Thanks.
DESDEMONA	But tell me more of life in Academe.
	If there be *cannibals that each other eat,*
	and men whose heads do grow beneath their
	shoulders?
	These things to hear, I seriously incline.
CONSTANCE	It is quite dog eat dog. And scary too.
	I've slaved for years to get my doctorate,
	but in a field like mine that's so well trod,
	you run the risk of contradicting men
	who've risen to the rank of sacred cow,
	and dying on the horns of those who rule
	the pasture with an iron cud.
	Not that I'm some kind of feminist.
	I shave my legs and I get nervous in a crowd –
	it's just that ... I was labelled as a crackpot,
	by the sacred herd of Academe;
	and after years spent as a laughingstock,
	I finally came to think that it was true.
	But, Desdemona, now that I've met you,
	I want to stand out in that field and cry, 'Bullshit!'
DESDEMONA	Wherefore? And what, pray tell, may bullshit be?
CONSTANCE	A kind of lie. For instance, Academe
	believes that you're a doomed and helpless victim.

DESDEMONA	I?
CONSTANCE	Ay.
DESDEMONA	Did I not beat a path into the fray,

DESDEMONA   Did I not beat a path into the fray,
my vow to honour in thy fool's cap quest?
Did I not flee my father, here to dwell
beneath the sword Hephaestus forged for Mars?
Will I not dive into Sargasso Sea,
to serve abreast the Amazons abroad?
Will I not butcher any cow that dares
low lies to call me tame, ay that I will!
So raise I now the battle cry, *Bullshit!!*

CONSTANCE &
DESDEMONA   *Bullshit!!! Bullshit!!! Bullshit!!!*

CONSTANCE   You are magnificent!
Othello should make you his lieutenant.
You're capable of greatness, Desdemona.
[*Enter the* SOLDIER]

SOLDIER   What ho! What ho! What ho! What ho! What ho!
Othello, warrior and raconteur,
would see my lady pedant post-post-haste,
in discourse touching secrets of the state.

CONSTANCE   Oh, okay. Bye.

DESDEMONA   Commend me to my lord.
[IAGO *enters as* CONSTANCE *and the* SOLDIER *exit. He sneaks up behind* DESDEMONA *with his bucket. She sniffs the air*]
What putrefaction haunts the island air?
Belike the slaughtered entrails of our meal?

IAGO   My lady.

DESDEMONA   O Iago! And so low?

IAGO   But that the love I bear my lord forbids,
I'd howl of treachery that tumbled me
from officer, to sweeper of his sewers.

DESDEMONA   Nay, speak.

IAGO	Since you command it, ma'am, I will:
	Once prowled I o'er the battlements, a proud
	protective beast to prey upon my lord's
	fell foes. Now creep I fetid conduits,
	to paw the slime, a declawed panther, trapped.
	And by a cunning mouse.
DESDEMONA	What rodent, this?
IAGO	Was that the Academic with you now?
DESDEMONA	It was.
IAGO	And called in private haste unto my Lord?
DESDEMONA	He makes of her his Delphic prophetess.
	Othello said she knows our secret selves.
IAGO	*Indeed?*
DESDEMONA	*Indeed? Ay, indeed. Discernst thou aught in that?*
	Is she not honest?
IAGO	*Honest,* madam?
DESDEMONA	*Honest? Ay, honest.*
IAGO	*For aught I know.*
DESDEMONA	*What dost thou think?*
IAGO	*Think, my lady?*
DESDEMONA	*Think, my lady?*
	By heaven, thou echoest me. Thou dost mean
	something.
	If thou dost love me, show me thy thought.
IAGO	M'lady, *you know I love you.*
DESDEMONA	*I think thou dost.*
	Therefore these stops of thine fright me the more.
IAGO	*It were not for your quiet nor your good,*
	to let you know my thoughts.
DESDEMONA	*By heaven, I'll know thy thoughts!*
IAGO	Beware my lady, of the mouse who eats
	the lion's cheese while sitting in his lap.
DESDEMONA	… cheese? … mouse? – lion? – in his lap? … to eat
	there? – What?!

	Think'st thou I'd make a life of jealousy?
IAGO	I would I did suspect mere harlotry.
DESDEMONA	Go to, thou knave!

[DESDEMONA *goes to strike* IAGO]

IAGO	*O monstrous world! Take note, take note, O world,*
	to be direct and honest is not safe.

[*He goes to exit*]

DESDEMONA	*Nay stay. Thou shouldst be honest.*
IAGO	I obey.
DESDEMONA	*And give the worst of thoughts the worst of words.*
IAGO	*The super-subtle* Academic spurned
	Othello's watch-dog [*refers to self*] from his naked
	side.
DESDEMONA	If the pedant be a judge of dog flesh,
	it was Othello who cashiered the cur.
IAGO	She lacks a husband.
DESDEMONA	So?
	'Tis vestal study that anoints her chaste.
IAGO	Pray God she be not secretly married.
DESDEMONA	*What dost thou mean?*
IAGO	A hag may seem a maid,
	when she in truth is Satan's bride.
DESDEMONA	A witch?
IAGO	She hath uncanny knowledge of our lives.
DESDEMONA	She spake of conjuring. And names for God,
	unknown to Christian ears. Of Amazons,
	who brook no men and live alone. Of mice –
IAGO	– her own familiar spirits.
DESDEMONA	Of men, that she changed into sacred cows.
IAGO	And so did Circe turn Ulysses' friends
	to pigs by witchcraft after she had lain with them.
DESDEMONA	She's with Othello now; ye stars forfend,
	he be not changed by suppertime! I'll hence!
IAGO	Stay ma'am! That is but half her purpose here.

Doth not the pedant prate of fool's cap?

DESDEMONA *Indeed.*

IAGO   *Indeed?* Of fool's cap she doth prate?

DESDEMONA It is a boon, that I am honour-bound to find.
I swore upon my life, this to perform.

IAGO The devil thus recruits an honest heart.
What's writ upon the fool's cap, in what tongue?

DESDEMONA A foreign tongue that's known to her alone.

IAGO What if it be an incantation, wrought
by infidels?   *magic spell*

DESDEMONA   I saw her read their script.
If it be that —

IAGO *If it be that, or any* heathen tongue,
it speaks against her with the other proofs.

DESDEMONA Is she an evil witch they have employed
to conjure up our secrets to their ears?!

IAGO The Turk did strike the hour she arrived.

DESDEMONA *O that the slave had forty thousand lives.*
One is too poor, too weak for my revenge!
O why did I embrace her as my friend?!
'Tis monstrous, O!!

IAGO *I see this hath a little dashed your spirits.*

DESDEMONA *Not a jot.* I'll to my lord and dilate all.

IAGO Hold! My lord's bewitched and hates me now;
he'll not believe.

DESDEMONA   Then how should we proceed?

IAGO Be not forsworn. Fulfill thy boon to her:
recover her unholy foolish cap,
her guilt to prove before you strike.

DESDEMONA   And proving
guilt,
I'll spit her head upon a pike *for daws to peck at.*
Thou wilt instruct me in the manly work
of sword-play; doubtless she is expert there,

for all her lack-a-liver timid show!

IAGO   *Patience, I say. Your mind may change.*

DESDEMONA   As well it may. La donn' e mobilé.

IAGO   [*alarmed*] *Yet watch her* ma'am, *if thou hast eyes to
            see.*
            She did deceive her Queens; *and she may thee.*

[CONSTANCE *and* OTHELLO *enter in conversation,
unaware of* DESDEMONA *and* IAGO *who draw back to listen, observe, and comment aside*]

OTHELLO   As thou dost love me, not a word of this
            to Desdemona. She must not suspect.

CONSTANCE   Don't worry, it will be our little secret.

[*They chuckle.* DESDEMONA *lunges forward but* IAGO
pulls her back]

DESDEMONA   *Look how she laughs already!*

[OTHELLO *takes out a large version of the velvet box that
Professor Night had in Act I, Scene i*]

OTHELLO   Which jewels most delight your female eye?

CONSTANCE   Diamonds, of course; a girl's best friend.

[OTHELLO *opens the box, takes out a diamond necklace
with a prominent gold clasp and places it around* CON-
STANCE'*s neck*]

DESDEMONA   Festoons the whore with baubles!

OTHELLO   The bees of Solomon ne'er counselled half so wise.
            Unto thy sweet and hiving breast,
            do I confide the honey of my heart.

DESDEMONA   Drone on my husband, drone. Thinkst thou to prick
            the queen? Ha! She would fain sting thee!;
            thereafter soon to die.

CONSTANCE   Don't mention it.

OTHELLO   Have I e'er told thee of the time I slew
            a singing beast in Turkish Antioch?
            'Twas on a grassy river bank where grazed
            a golden ox. The beast did tend this ox.

Three heads grew from the shoulders of the beast.
On one the hair was black as ebony,
the other crown was curl'ed angel fair,
the third head wore a scarlet cap of wool,
that ended in a foolish bauble bright.
I asked the beast to show the shallow spot
where it was wont to ford the ox of gold.

CONSTANCE In some strange way this beast seems so familiar.

IAGO 'Familiar'! Yet again 'familiar'!
Most potent witch to suckle such a beast!

CONSTANCE You say you killed it dead?

OTHELLO   The demon fell
and bled a sea of inky green.

CONSTANCE   Alas.

DESDEMONA She mourns a beast of Turkish Antioch!

OTHELLO I left the thing for dead, as I made haste
to find a shallow spot and ford my ox.

CONSTANCE Your ox? Ford, your ox? [*aside*] I'm having déjà-vu.
I think we'd better leave each other now.
Your wife may come and think that something's up.

IAGO We know what's up, and who will soon go down.

DESDEMONA Adultress! Let me stone her in the square!

OTHELLO Adieu friend, I'll have more of thee anon.

[OTHELLO *embraces* CONSTANCE *vigorously*]

IAGO *As prime as goats, as hot as monkeys.*

[OTHELLO *releases* CONSTANCE *and goes to exit. He stops,
sniffs the air*]

OTHELLO Iago?

IAGO [*emerging from the shadows*] My lord.

OTHELLO Look to the morning's night-soil. And keep in the light.

IAGO Yes my Lord.

[OTHELLO *pats* CONSTANCE *on the head*]

CONSTANCE [*to* OTHELLO] 'Night 'night.

[*As* OTHELLO *exits,* CONSTANCE *sees* IAGO *whisper to*

DESDEMONA *before he too exits.* CONSTANCE *conceals the necklace*]

DESDEMONA   Academic!

CONSTANCE   Oh, Desdemona – hi. I've been meaning to ask you, does Lord Othello keep a Wise Fool here?

DESDEMONA   The only wise fool is a one that's dead.
I hate a tripping, singing, licensed fool,
that makes a motley of the mighty,
and profanes the sacred with base parody.

CONSTANCE   Oh.
[DESDEMONA *glowers at* CONSTANCE]
Are you okay?

DESDEMONA   *I have a pain upon my forehead, here.*

CONSTANCE   Tsk, tsk, tsk, well I'm not surprised. I saw you talking to that creep, Iago –

DESDEMONA   'Creep'?

CONSTANCE   Colloquial for, 'base and noisome knave.'
I'd stay away from him if I were you.

DESDEMONA   Wherefore? Hast thou some secret knowledge of him?

CONSTANCE   Oh yes. You'd be surprised how much I know.

DESDEMONA   I think not. I think thou know'st my husband.

CONSTANCE   I know some things I hope you'll never know.

DESDEMONA   What passed between my lord and thee just now?

CONSTANCE   Uh-oh. What did you hear?

DESDEMONA   Enough to rear suspicion's head.

CONSTANCE   Oh no.

DESDEMONA   O yes!

CONSTANCE   Oh well.
Whate'er you do, don't let him know that you suspect.

DESDEMONA   Nay, he'll know not that I wot aught.
[*aside*] *Goats and monkeys!*

[DESDEMONA *goes to exit*]

CONSTANCE   Boy, Shakespeare really watered her down, eh?...
I wish I were more like Desdemona.
Next to her I'm just a little wimp.
A rodent. Road-kill. Furry tragedy
all squashed and steaming on the 401
with 'Michelin' stamped all over me. It's true:
people've always made a fool of me
without my even knowing. Gullible.
That's me. Old Connie. Good sport. Big joke. Ha.
Just like that time at recess in grade five:
a gang of bully girls comes up to me.
Their arms are linked, they're chanting as they
    march,
'Hey. Hey. Get outta my way!
I just got back from the I.G.A.!'
I'm terrified. They pin me down,
and force me to eat a dog-tongue sandwich.
I now know it was only ham ...
O, what would Desdemona do to Claude,
had she *the motive and the cue for passion
that I have?* She would drown all Queen's with
    blood,
and cleave Claude Night's two typing fingers from
his guilty hands. She'd wrap them in a box
of choc'lates and present them to Ramona.
She'd kill him in cold blood and in blank verse,
then smear the ivied walls in scarlet letters spelling
    'thief'!
To think, I helped him use me: a gull, a stooge,
a swine adorned with mine own pearls,
a sous-chef, nay! a scull'ry-maid that slaved
to heat hell's kitchen with the baking stench
of forty-thousand scalding humble-pies,

O Vengeance!!!

[DESDEMONA *and* IAGO *enter, sword-fighting.* IAGO *disarms* DESDEMONA, *his sword poised to strike.* CONSTANCE *snatches up* DESDEMONA'*s sword and thrusts savagely and repeatedly at* IAGO *with:*]

    Villainy, villainy, villainy!

[CONSTANCE *disarms* IAGO, *knocks him down and is poised to skewer him*]

    May thy pernicious soul rot half a grain a day!

[*She raises her sword to strike, but* DESDEMONA *stops her*]

DESDEMONA Hold!

[DESDEMONA *helps* IAGO *to his feet. He glares at* CONSTANCE, *shaken*]

    'Twas all in sport.

CONSTANCE Oh.

IAGO Ay.

CONSTANCE Gee. I'm sorry. Um – [*to* IAGO] here's your sword back and everything ... [*retreating*] Have fun.

    [*aside*] Dear God, I could have murdered that poor
      man.
    I saw a flash of red before my eyes.
    I felt a rush of power through my veins.
    I tasted iron blood inside my mouth.
    I loved it!

[CONSTANCE *faints*]

DESDEMONA   *If she be false, heaven mocked itself.*

[*holding her sword at* IAGO'*s throat*]

    Wretch, *be sure thou prove* my friend a villainess!
    Be sure of it; give me the ocular proof –

[IAGO *manages to take the Manuscript page from his shirt*]

IAGO   *Yet be content!*

DESDEMONA   *Make me to see't!*

[IAGO *thrusts the page under her nose*]

                What's this?

IAGO   The pedant's fool's cap writ in Turkish code, found by
       my wife in your underwear drawer!
       [DESDEMONA *releases* IAGO]

DESDEMONA   *Damn her, lewd spy! O damn her, damn her, O!*

IAGO   *O, 'tis foul in her.*

DESDEMONA   *And to lie with my* husband!

IAGO   *That's fouler.*

DESDEMONA   Fool's cap – *confession* – fool's cap – *to confess then die –*
       first to die, then to confess –   ~~sudden loss of~~
                                           ~~conscious~~
       [DESDEMONA *is about to fall prey to apoplexy when*
       CONSTANCE *wakes up and picks something off the hem of*
       DESDEMONA *'s dress*]

CONSTANCE   My Brownie wings! What are they doing here?
       I thought I threw them in the garb … age. Oh.

DESDEMONA   [*aside*] *She may be honest yet.* I'll try her once
       in fairness. Then *I'll chop her into messes.*
       [DESDEMONA *impales the foolscap upon the point of her
       sword*]

CONSTANCE   Hey Desdemona! Look what I just found.
       My Brown Owl wings!

IAGO   [*aside to* DESDEMONA] An owl stands for a witch!
       It is the shape that Hecate takes at night.

DESDEMONA   I know who thou art. And I saw what thou didst.

CONSTANCE   You mean you've found out who I really am?
       [DESDEMONA *nods*]
       Who?! Who?! Who?!

IAGO   The owl's cry!
       [DESDEMONA *points her sword with the foolscap, at*
       CONSTANCE *'s face*]

DESDEMONA   Here is the sword of justice. If this be thine,
       read the verdict and reveal thyself.

CONSTANCE   It certainly looks like the real McCoy.
       [CONSTANCE *plucks the foolscap off the sword*]
       It is! Page one! I must be getting warm.

[*reads*] 'Thou'rt cold, and Cyprus is too hot for thee.
Seek truth now in Verona, Italy;
there find a third to make a trinity,
where two plus one adds up to one not three.'
Hm. How strange.
[*Warp effects.* CONSTANCE *starts to be pulled off.* DES-
DEMONA *grabs her by the skirt. When the warp effects are
over, all that remains of Constance is her skirt which is
speared onto* DESDEMONA*'s sword*]

DESDEMONA   The pedant hath by magic disappeared
to fly unto her evil genius, Brown Owl.
When she returns with fresh enchantments here,
then must the cause of justice claim her life.
How shall I kill her Iago?
[IAGO *hands* DESDEMONA *the pillow*]

Act III, Scene i. ❧

Verona; a public place.
MERCUTIO *and* TYBALT *are about to fight.* ROMEO *looks
on, horrified.*

MERCUTIO   [*draws*] *Tybalt, you ratcatcher, will you walk?*
TYBALT   [*draws*] *I am for you.*
ROMEO   *Gentle Mercutio, put thy rapier up.*
MERCUTIO   *Come sir, your passado!*
[*They fight.* CONSTANCE *enters, minus her skirt, now
wearing just her longjohns, boots and tweed jacket*]
ROMEO   *Hold, Tybalt! Good Mercutio!*
[ROMEO *is about to fatally intervene in the sword fight*]
CONSTANCE   [*aside*] One Mona Lisa down, and one to go.
[*She tackles* ROMEO*. They fly into the sword fight, knocking
*TYBALT *and* MERCUTIO *aside.* TYBALT *and* MERCUTIO

jump to their feet and immediately point their swords at
CONSTANCE *while* ROMEO *sits on her*]

MERCUTIO   Shall I lance the pimple? Or rub the quat
             to bursting!

TYBALT   Name the house that whelped thee pup!
             What kennel loosed thee hence to interfere
             with honour's reck'ning?

ROMEO   [*to* TYBALT *and* MERCUTIO] Stay! You fright the
             wretch.
             Speak, boy ... speak boy.

CONSTANCE   [*aside*] Boy?

[*a moment of decision. She clears her throat to a more masculine pitch*]

                         From Cyprus washed I here ashore,
             a roving pedant lad to earn my bread
             by wit and by this fountain pen, my sword.
             A stranger here, my name is Constan- ... tine.
             I couldn't let you kill each other for,
             young Juliet and Romeo have wed;
             and by th'untying of their virgin-knot,
             have tied new blood betwixt you cousins here.
             Tybalt, Romeo is your cousin now,
             in law, and so you fellows should shake hands.

[*A dangerous pause, then* TYBALT *turns to* ROMEO *and embraces him*]

TYBALT   Cousin Montague!
ROMEO   Kindred Capulet!

[MERCUTIO *and* TYBALT *embrace* CONSTANCE *in turn with:*]

TYBALT   Fortunate harbinger!
MERCUTIO   Madcap youth!
ROMEO   Brave Greek!

[ROMEO *embraces* CONSTANCE, *but lingers a little too long with:*]

[*aside*] *Did my heart love till now?* Forswear it, nay!
For I ne'er saw true beauty till this day!

MERCUTIO Now we have put our angry weapons up,
let's hie to Mistress Burnbottom's to put up
and to sheath our jocund tools of sport.
[*Lewd Renaissance gestures and laughter throughout the
following dreadful jokes*]

TYBALT A bawd! And falling apart with'th' pox! Take care –
She'll pay *thee,* and with a French crown too!

MERCUTIO Ay, a bald pate, for a little head!

TYBALT I'd as lief to pluck a green maid off the street.

MERCUTIO Thou'dst feel that green fruit yerking in thy guts,
when that her kinsfolk 'venge her maidenhead!

TYBALT She'd never know who'd had her maidenhead,
for I would pass as quickly through the wench,
as any fruit so green, would pass through me!
[*Laughter –* CONSTANCE *nervously bites her thumb-nail*]
Do you bite your thumb at me sir?!

CONSTANCE No! I just bite my nails, that's all.

TYBALT Do you bite your nails at me sir?!

CONSTANCE No I swear! Look, I'll never bite them again. This'll be a
great chance for me to quit once and for all. Thanks.
[*Pause. The boys tense. Will there be a fight?*]

TYBALT You're welcome.

ROMEO Now t'th' baths, new friendship to baptize!

MERCUTIO &
TYBALT T'th' baths, t'th' baths!

ROMEO   [*to* CONSTANCE] Come
Greekling, splash with us!
[ROMEO, TYBALT *and* MERCUTIO *hoist* CONSTANCE
onto their shoulders]

CONSTANCE No, wait! I can't! I had a bath today.
[*struggling down*] What's more, I've got a lot of
things to do;

I have to buy a lute, a sword, some hose,
and teach a class or two before it's noon,
in time to see a man about a horse.
ROMEO   I'd see thee mounted well in stallion flesh.
Beware thou art deceived not in a mare.
[ROMEO, TYBALT *and* MERCUTIO *exit*]
CONSTANCE Thank God they think that I'm a man. [*to God*] Thank
you. O thank you.
How long can I avoid their locker room?
Those guys remind me of the Stratford shows I've
    seen,
where each production has a Roman bath:
the scene might be a conference of state,
but steam will rise and billow from the wings,
while full-grown men in Velcro loin-cloths speak,
while snapping towels at each other.
Why is it Juliet's scenes with her Nurse
are never in a sauna. Or 'King Lear':
imagine Goneril and Regan, steaming
as they plot the downfall of their Dad,
while tearing hot wax from each other's legs;
Ophelia, drowning in a whirlpool full
of naked women. Portia, pumping iron –
[*A woman screams within. Male laughter*]
[*verge of tears*] I want to go home.
I want to see my cats. I want to read
'Jane Eyre' again and never leave the house.
Where's the Fool? Where's the damn Fool?!
How come I end up doing all his work?
I should have waited in the wings
for him to leap on stage and stop the fight,
and then I could have pinned him down
and forced him to reveal the Author's name!
The Author – who must know my true identity.

The Author! who – I have to pee …
There must be a convent around here somewhere.
[*Exit* CONSTANCE]

Act III, Scene ii.

Juliet and Romeo's bedchamber.
The next day. Bright sunlight. Oppressive heat. JULIET, *clad in a Renaissance peignoir set, languishes near the bed and fans herself, while* ROMEO *sleeps.*

JULIET *Ay me.* [*yawn*]
ROMEO [*half-asleep*] *Was that the lark?*
JULIET It was the luncheon bell.
ROMEO Oh no! [*leaps out of bed*]
Julie-e-et, where be my blue doublet?!
JULIET Under the bed where thou didst leave it, dear.
[ROMEO *retrieves his doublet*]
JULIET & ROMEO [*both aside*] Th'affections of our love's first-sighted blood,
have in the cauldron of one hot swift night,
all cooled to creeping jelly in the pot.
JULIET *Wilt thou be gone?*
ROMEO [*on with the doublet*] Yes dear. There's some fun going forward at The Gondolier: the fellows and I are getting up a cock-fight, followed by a bear-baiting, then hie us to a public hanging in the piazza, there to take our noon-day meal. [*aside*] I mean to find the lovely Greek boy, Constantine, or die.
JULIET Goodbye dear.
ROMEO Goodbye.

[ROMEO *exits on the run, but stops short just outside*]
Zounds! I had forgot.
[*He heads back into the chamber*]
What Julie-e-et!
JULIET   What?
[ROMEO *is frantically searching for something*]
ROMEO   Where be Hector, my turtle?
JULIET   Belike dead in the chamber pot.
ROMEO   [*verge of tears*] Dead?! My Hector?!
JULIET   [*verge of tears*] Dead?! Sayest thou?!
ROMEO   Nay, thou sayest so!
JULIET   Nay, I know not. Perchance he lives yet in the water dish.
[ROMEO *and* JULIET *both dash to the water dish and retrieve Hector the turtle, whom they share between their two cupped hands*]
ROMEO   Poseidon be thanked! Hector lives to fight another day!
JULIET   Be Lazarus from this day forth, thou risen turtle.
[*They shower the turtle with loving kisses*]
ROMEO   [*to* JULIET] I must be gone.
[*They exchange a cursory peck on the cheek*]
JULIET   Goodbye dear.
ROMEO   Goodbye dear.
[ROMEO *attempts to exit with Hector*]
Let go thy hand, for I must needs be gone,
and Hector goes with me.
JULIET   Nay, stays with me.
ROMEO   He goes.
JULIET   He stays!
[*A turtle tug-of-war ensues*]
ROMEO   Goes!
JULIET   Stays!
ROMEO   Goes!
[*Hector is ripped in two*]
JULIET   Ah! Hector! *Look how he bleeds!*

ROMEO   *Warm and new killed.* O Hector. O heavens!
         [*They weep*]
JULIET   Thou bloody-fingered boy, hast slaughtered him!
ROMEO   Thou panther-taloned girl, hast rent his shell!
JULIET   I'll tell my father!
ROMEO   So will I tell mine!
         O wherefore did I wive a sniv'lling girl?!
         [ROMEO *exits in tears*]
JULIET   O wherefore married I a stripling boy?!
         [NURSE *calls from within*]
NURSE   *What Juliet, ladybird,* what little maid!
JULIET   [*aside*] No maid but matron, thus made and
             unmade.
         [NURSE *enters. She is hot and puffing, and carries a gift-
         wrapped package*]
NURSE   Another wedding gift for thee my lamb.
         Beshrew this heat, Verona is ablaze!
         'T'will be tomorrow fourteen years ago
         since thou wert born upon a wave of heat
         that cooked the country, marry, to an ash.
         Child look, I have a pretty box for thee.
         [JULIET *doesn't look up*]
JULIET   Say if it take the measure of my corpse?
NURSE   Nay, 'tis no bigger than a bread chest.
JULIET   Entomb it with the rest and leave me be,
         and when thou hast done so, come weep with me,
         past hope, past care, past help, past tense, O Nurse!!!
         [JULIET *flings herself upon* NURSE*'s bosom and sobs*]
NURSE   There, there, lamb, thou art too soon made a bride.
         Was Cupid's loving dart too sharp for thee?
         Say if Romeo's of unnatural size,
         to tear [*as in 'tear drop'*] thee so? Or mayhap, saints
             forfend,
         behind his boyish drool there lurks a foaming wolf!

A pox on him! Though't be thy wifely load,
to bear his married weight, I'll pry him hence,
with false chancres for thy nether lips.

JULIET　Oh Nurse, 'tis none of these!

NURSE　　　　　　　　　　　　　What is it then?

JULIET　I die of tedium!

NURSE　Oh.

JULIET　O Hymen, god of marriage, pray undo
thy holy work: Make me a maid again!
To plunge once more in love's first firey pit,
to hover there 'twixt longing and content,
condemned to everlasting Limbo, O!
Penance me with new love's burning tongs;
spit and sear me slow o'er heaven's flames;
grant me an eternity to play with fire!

NURSE　By my maid'nhead, what a turn is here.

JULIET　O, I have naught to live for from today;
a once-plucked rose that withers ere it's blown;
tomorrow sees the change of fourteen years,
yet even now my life is ended.

NURSE　　　　　　　　　　　　Nay.
There's much to live for yet.

JULIET　　　　　　　　　　　　Name one of much.

NURSE　This very night thy wedding feast invites
Verona to a table that doth groan
with joy, and creak at new-fit joinery
of married Capulet and Montague.

JULIET　[*subsiding sobs*] A party? Tonight? I had forgot.

NURSE　Be merry. Feast thine eyes on fresh gallants;
rekindle loving embers to re-heat
thy day-old husband when the feast is o'er.

JULIET　I will look. And yet not seek to touch.
Thanks Nurse. [*aside*] But touched and whetted
　　once before,

love's first keen edge grows dull with use and craves
another grinding. [*to* NURSE] Nurse, what shall I
wear?

Act III, Scene iii. 🌺

A public place.
Enter CONSTANCE, *furtive, peering at someone, off.*

CONSTANCE I've found him. I've found the Fool. He's skulking
around here, carrying a bag full of Manuscript pages.
[CONSTANCE *lurks apart, as a strangely dressed* SERVANT
*enters with a bag full of foolscap scrolls outwardly identical
to the Manuscript pages*]
[*aside*] I suppose I could just ask him … no: 'When in
Verona –'
[CONSTANCE *pounces on him and pins him down*]
Name the Author, thou elusive Fool!
What fiendish hack is he that scribbled thee
and these [*scrolls*] and this [*this world*] unto the light
of day?!

SERVANT Don't hurt me sir, pray hurt me not and I will talk.

CONSTANCE I'm listening.

SERVANT *My master is the great rich Capulet* and he hath writ all
that you see.

CONSTANCE Juliet's father, Capulet?
[*the* SERVANT *nods*]
Wrote all this? [*she regards the scrolls*] Wow.
[CONSTANCE *unrolls the scroll and – with great
expectation – looks at it. But there is no warp. She riffles the
other scrolls*]
These are just party invitations.

SERVANT Ay.

CONSTANCE [*reading aloud*] 'Signor Capulet is pleased to announce the marriage of his daughter, Juliet, to Romeo of Montague, and doth request the honour of your company at a masked ball this night.' You're not the Fool.

SERVANT Thank you, sir.

CONSTANCE [*to herself*] A masked ball for Romeo … and Juliet … 'a third to make a trinity' … I've got to buy a mask! [*to the* SERVANT] Can you lend me a few ducats?

Act III, Scene iv. ❦

That night. The masked wedding feast at Capulet Hall. Renaissance party sounds, decorations, a roast suckling pig with apple … Everyone wears a half-mask. Enter ROMEO *and* JULIET, *sulky and annoyed with each other. The* SERVANT *sings a love song and plays a lute.* JULIET *scrutinizes him. The song ends.*

JULIET Boy, wherefore is thy voice so sweet and high?

SERVANT For that I sing castrato, lady.

JULIET Oh. Hast thou a brother that's a tenor?

SERVANT Ay ma'am. [*points off*] Look where he tunes his instrument.

JULIET [*exiting*] So tune I mine, to pitch in sweet duet.

ROMEO If only Constantine were here tonight;
this feast were better borne in light of him.
I feigned a mirthful splashing at the baths,
and sought, but could not find him out today.
What if he's gone and barked again for Greece?
If this be so, I'll to my closet straight,
there to forswear all daylight and all food,
to mirror thus the wasting of my heart,
all shrouded in the dark night of my soul.

[*Enter* TYBALT, *masked.* ROMEO *approaches him from behind*]

    [*aside*] No mask can hide that sleek Aegean form.

    This is my Constant-teen as I am his.

[ROMEO *places his hand on* TYBALT's *bottom.* TYBALT *whirls about, yanks* ROMEO's *eye mask forward, and lets it snap back when he recognizes him*]

TYBALT   Ah, Romeo, 'tis thee my cuz!

[TYBALT *gives* ROMEO *a macho slap on the ass and laughs*]

ROMEO   Tybalt!

    I knew 'twas thee.

[ROMEO *punches* TYBALT, *jock-like, on the arm. The friendly brutality goes on until* ROMEO *sees* CONSTANCE *enter, wearing a stupid Mouse half-mask*]

    I'll pummel thee to pulp anon, my cuz,

    but now must I put on the gentle host.

[ROMEO *leaves* TYBALT *and cautiously approaches* CONSTANCE. TYBALT *exits*]

    Constantine?

CONSTANCE Romeo?

ROMEO Ay!

CONSTANCE Hi.

[ROMEO *embraces* CONSTANCE *warmly, taking her off guard*]

    Oh. [*extricating herself*] Heh.

[ROMEO *gazes into her eyes*]

    Um. How do you like being married?

ROMEO Speak not of Juliet, 'tis thee I love.

CONSTANCE What?

[ROMEO *drops to one knee and seizes her hand*]

ROMEO   O Constantine, O emperor of my heart!

    It is my sex that is thine enemy.

    Call me but love, and I'll be new endowed.

CONSTANCE It isn't that – good grief, get up.

ROMEO Then love me!

[*He jumps up to kiss her.* CONSTANCE *escapes*]

CONSTANCE No, please, I – I'm not that kind of boy.

ROMEO What kind of boy?

CONSTANCE The kind that can just hop right into bed
with any Tom or Dick or … Romeo.

ROMEO Where be these rivals, Tom and Dick?!
Are their sweet lips more to thy taste than mine?

CONSTANCE Oh no, I … suspect that you're beyond compare.

ROMEO Then kiss me now and prove suspicion true.
Surrender unto Romeo thy lips,
and let him enter at those ruby gates,
forever barred against both Tom and Dick.

CONSTANCE [*about to yield*] Oh my.

[*Enter* TYBALT, *jovial, drinking a Coors Light*]

TYBALT [*aside*] I'm told the Greek boy, Constantine, doth feast
with us tonight. [*sees* CONSTANCE] Ah.

[ROMEO *kisses* CONSTANCE*'s neck*]

[*aside*] O! What, an Hellenic deviant?! O fie!

CONSTANCE Please, Romeo, you don't understand, I can't do this, I'm
not – I'm – way too old for you!

ROMEO A maiden blush bepaints thy hairless cheek.
[*he strokes her cheek*]
Eternal springs the fountain of thy youth;
I'd quench myself at thy Priapic font.
[*he kisses her neck*]

CONSTANCE O … Romeo …

TYBALT [*aside*] And dares this mockery of manhood bent,
come hither, covered with an antic face,
to fleer and lisp at our solemnity?

CONSTANCE Romeo, please, I know your family – they'll be very
upset.

ROMEO Boy, *what love can do, that dares love attempt.*
Therefore my kinsmen are no stop to me.

CONSTANCE   They are to me! I'm not a hero, I'm just a school teacher.
ROMEO   And my Socrates that art condemned
            in sweet subversion of Verona's youth.
            Then die thou not alone. *I'll kiss thy lips.*
            Haply some hemlock *yet doth hang on them.*
CONSTANCE   I don't want to die! –
ROMEO   O that I were a fountain pen within thy hand,
            to spurt forth streams of eloquence at thy command!
            [ROMEO *kisses* CONSTANCE. *She yields*]
TYBALT   [*aside*] The villain! He is hither come in spite,
            to shame my cousin, Romeo, this night.
            [*Enter* JULIET, *dishevelled.* TYBALT *hides his rage. The kiss
            ends*]   disorder
            [*to* JULIET] Gentle cuz, pray rescue Romeo;
            he's trapped in tedious discourse with that man.
JULIET   Romeo, a messenger doth cry.
ROMEO   Perchance he cries for thee, dear.
CONSTANCE   [*awestruck*] Juliet?
JULIET   Ay.
ROMEO   Juliet, this be Constantine, the Greek –
            blind Cupid's servant, who unveiled our love
            for all the world to see.
JULIET   Oh. Thanks.
            [*aside*] The Greek hath taught not just the world to
                see,
            but also me. Would I were blind again.
            [CONSTANCE *removes her mask and extends her hand*]
CONSTANCE   I'm truly thrilled to meet you, Juliet.
JULIET   [*aside*] Hail, Roman Cupid that hath heard my cries,
            and sent Greek Eros to benight mine eyes!
            [JULIET *takes* CONSTANCE'*s hand and does not release it*]
            [*to* ROMEO] Romeo, a man doth steal thy horse
                within.
            [*Exit* ROMEO, *alarmed. Music.* JULIET *leads* CON-

STANCE *in a dance throughout the following dialogue*]
Romeo spake of thee as pedant wise.

CONSTANCE I wouldn't say I'm really all that wise.
I have done lots of homework on you, though.
For years I've sought to penetrate your source,
and dreamt of meeting you a thousand times –

JULIET Awake. Or let me share thy sleep of dreams.
I'd have thee penetrate my secret source,
and know me full as well and deep as thou
dost know thyself O dreamer, Constantine.

CONSTANCE There must be something in Verona's air;
I feel like half my years have dropped away.

JULIET The air is redolent with hearts afire;
their flames all licking at thy new-blown lip,
consume thy tongue to spark of love alone.

CONSTANCE Wow.
[JULIET *gives a little laugh.* CONSTANCE *giggles*]
May I ask you something?

JULIET   Anything.

CONSTANCE You're the essence of first love –
of beauty that will never fade,
of passion that will never die.
Are you afraid of growing old?

JULIET No one may remain forever young.
We change our swaddling clothes for funeral
    shrouds,
and in between is one brief shining space,
where love may strike by chance, but only death is
    sure.

CONSTANCE What happens though, if love itself should die?

JULIET When love goes to its grave before we do,
then find another love for whom to die,
and swear to end life first when next we love.

CONSTANCE So love is tragic, or it isn't love.

JULIET   The readiness to die doth crown true love,
                and is its richest living ornament.

CONSTANCE   And tears, not smiles, its truest measure ...

[*Enter* TYBALT *and* ROMEO *from different places*]

ROMEO   [*aside*] I rode not hither on a horse tonight!

TYBALT   [*aside re* CONSTANCE] O villain, that would plunder
                shirt and skirt!

ROMEO   [*aside re* CONSTANCE] How swingst thou now,
                capricious pendulum!

TYBALT   [*aside re* CONSTANCE] *Now, by the stock and honour
                of my kin,
                to strike him dead, I hold it not a sin.*

ROMEO   [*aside*] Then let a bodice be my winding sheet;
                I'll wear a woman's gown until I die,
                sith it's a piece of skirt that likes his eye!

[JULIET *and* CONSTANCE *dance by.* ROMEO *cuts in and
continues the dance with* CONSTANCE]

JULIET   [*aside*] I now perceive the slant of Constantine's
                desire.
                He looks to match his stick to light his fire.
                And since he savours a two-legg'ed pose,
                I'll into Romeo's closet and steal hose!

TYBALT   [*aside*] *I will withdraw; but this intrusion shall,
                now seeming sweet, convert to bitt'rest gall.*

[TYBALT *crushes his Coors Light can in his fist, tosses it at*
CONSTANCE'*s feet, and exits.* CONSTANCE *pauses in her
dance with* ROMEO, *picks up the can, and recognizes it*]

JULIET   [*aside*] Thou pretty boy, I will ungreek thee yet.
                [*intercepting* CONSTANCE]
                If I profane with my unworthiest hand –

ROMEO   Hold! I saw him first.

JULIET   Thou wouldst corrupt him.

ROMEO   Sayst *thou?!* Thou that bedded the first doublet
                to o'erperch thine orchard walls?

JULIET   Thou caitiff!
I sicken of thy blubb'ring boyish charm.

ROMEO   Thou'rt in the green-eyed clutch of envy, sweet.

JULIET   'Gather ye rosebuds while ye may,' Romeo,
for with each new lust, thou creepeth close
unto the ag'ed day when soft moist lip
and dewy eye convert to senile rheum.

ROMEO   Thinkst *thou* to leave a lovely corpse my dear,
when even now the crows have footed it
in merry measure all about thine eyes?

JULIET   Oh! I shall tell my father of this insult!

[*They are both on the verge of passionate tears*]

ROMEO   Be thou assured *my* father will hear of it!

CONSTANCE   You kids, now that's enough, just settle down,
involving family here will make things worse.

JULIET   [*weeping*] I wish I were dead!

ROMEO   [*weeping*] I wish I had ne'er been born!

CONSTANCE   Now, that's no way to talk. Apologize,
and count your lucky stars.

[ROMEO *and* JULIET *stare at* CONSTANCE *for a moment*]

ROMEO &
JULIET   [*to* CONSTANCE] Our lucky stars?

CONSTANCE I need a breath of air. Thanks for the party. It was a ball.
Shutup Constance.

[*Exit* CONSTANCE]

Act III, Scene v. ❧

Constance's balcony overlooking an orchard.
The SERVANT *warbles on the balcony, holding a taper.*
CONSTANCE *enters the balcony, sees something on the floor,*
bends down and picks up the Chorus's half-smoked cigarette
butt from her office. She lights her cigarette from the SER-

vant's *taper and inhales gratefully. Exit* SERVANT. *Enter* JULIET *below the balcony, dressed in Romeo's clothing.*

JULIET   *[below] But soft! What light through yonder*
    window breaks?
    It is the East, and Constantine *the sun!*

CONSTANCE   Uh oh.

JULIET   He speaks.

CONSTANCE   Romeo? Is that you?

JULIET   *I know not how to tell thee who I am.*
    My sex, dear boy, *is hateful to myself,*
    because it is belov'ed not by thee;
    therefore I wear tonight, this boyish hose.

CONSTANCE   Juliet? What are you doing down there? How on earth did you get into the orchard?

JULIET   *With love's light wings did i o'erperch* —

CONSTANCE   I see.
    I'm sorry Juliet, it's not to be,
    I'm not at all the man you think I am.

JULIET   I wot well what thou art, and yet I love.

CONSTANCE   You do?

JULIET   Ay.

CONSTANCE   You mean you know my true identity?

JULIET   Indeed. Thou art a deviant of Greece.
    O Constantine! O wherefore art thou bent?

CONSTANCE   Shshshsh! Good Heavens, keep your voice down please.

JULIET   Deny thy preference and refuse thy sex;
    Or, if thou wilt not, be but sworn my love,
    and henceforth never will I be a girl.

CONSTANCE   I'm not … a deviant, for heaven's sake.

JULIET   Not deviant? Art thou then a timid virgin?
    Dear boy, I envy thee thy bliss to come.

CONSTANCE   I may be celibate, but I'm not exactly a virgin.

JULIET   Tut, boyish bluster. Hast thou tasted woman?

CONSTANCE   No!

JULIET   Then are thy vestal senses all intact.
O let Juliet initiate
thy budding taste of woman's dewy rose.
Learn how the rose becomes a sea of love:
come part the waves and plumb Atlantic depths.
I'll guide thee to the oyster's precious pearl ...
we'll seek out wat'ry caves for glist'ning treasure,
spelunk all night until we die of pleasure.

CONSTANCE   I'm not into that sort of thing. _a pipe for fluids to run through_

JULIET   Then claim another conduit for thy use.

CONSTANCE   Heavenly days, what's come over you?!
You're supposed to be all innocence.

JULIET   The time for innocence is sped!
I'll love once more before I'm dead!

CONSTANCE   Who said anything about dying? You're only fourteen years old.

JULIET   Thirteen! Tomorrow will I be fourteen.

CONSTANCE   You will? So will I! I mean, be a year older.

JULIET   We share the self-same stars! We're truly matched.

CONSTANCE   Juliet?

JULIET   My love?

CONSTANCE   I'm flattered. And you're very beautiful,
and sweet and passionate, and probably
a – lovely ... lover, but – in point of fact,
I don't – I can't – I must – not. Love you. Juliet.

JULIET   Wherefore?

CONSTANCE   Well ... for one thing, you're married.

JULIET   Hmph.

CONSTANCE   And we've barely met.

JULIET   So?

CONSTANCE   I don't believe in love-at-first-sight.

JULIET   Say then that thou dost not believe in air!

Or in the solid ground on which we tread!
Nay, love's a force of nature, can't be stopped;
the lightning waiteth not upon my thought
to thus endow it bright; it doth but light!

CONSTANCE   Nay, love's a bond of servitude;
a trap that sly deceptors lay for fools –
fools they use then throw away,
or trade in like a lib'ry book
they've read, then lost, then found beneath the bed
all coffee-stained and dust-bunnied,
all dog-eared, thumbed and overdue.

JULIET   Thou art one that loved and lost.

CONSTANCE   Well. I will admit I had a crush –
delayed post-adolescent fantasy.

JULIET   Seek not to excuse thy one true love.

CONSTANCE   No. I refuse to say that I felt love
for someone who did grind my mind to pulp,
and lined a gilded bird-cage with the dust.
He played the parrot: I fed him great lines,
and he pooped on my head.   *did not return*

JULIET   Unrequited love.

CONSTANCE It certainly was unrequited: I never pooped back. I could
kick myself.   *a semi tropical*
                                          asian tree
JULIET   He crushed thy heart as 't'were a pomegranate
underfoot and thou didst kiss that foot.

CONSTANCE   [*starting to give in*] Yes.

JULIET   And doted on his every
whim.

CONSTANCE   Yes.

JULIET   And idolized him from the start.

CONSTANCE   I loved him from the moment I first saw him
across the crowded cafeteria.
He looked so dignified, and irritated.
I stood second in the line for lunch.

I saw him check his watch and pinch his nose.
'He has important things to do,' I thought,
and so I offered up my place to him.
He thanked me in his cultivated voice,
and asked where one might find a decent cup of tea.
I told him I'd be glad to make him one,
and shared with him the last of my Velveeta.
He smiled as he ate my cheese.
I loved that man ...

JULIET   Tell heaven!

CONSTANCE   [*meekly to heaven*] I loved Claude Night. Love.

JULIET   Declaim!

CONSTANCE   Love. Love! I love that shit, Claude Night!
Amour – at-first-sight, in plain view, a coup de
    foudre,
la vie en soir, amo, amas, amat!!!
There. I've said it. So what do I do now?

JULIET   Impale thy cleav'ed heart upon a sword!

CONSTANCE   Yes O yes!!! I wish I had the nerve
to do it right in front of everyone
while standing in the cafeteria line!;
to play a swan-song on my arteries,
anoint the daily special with my veins!

JULIET   [*offering dagger*] Stab thyself first, then will I stab
    mine!

CONSTANCE   Thanks. That's very sweet of you, Juliet.
But not just now. I have to find the Author first;
or else the Fool to lead me to the bard.

JULIET   Author? Fool?

CONSTANCE   And Self. It is my quest,
and it means more to me than love or death.

JULIET   What passion is of such ferocity?

CONSTANCE   The one that killed the cat: curiosity.

JULIET   I know the Author, Constantine.

CONSTANCE   You do?

JULIET   Ay. The Fool told me.

CONSTANCE   Who is he? What's his name?

JULIET   Wouldst love me if I told thee who it be?

CONSTANCE   Until I pass into another world.

JULIET   Mount unto my closet for a tryst.
        I'll trade the name, and claim of thee one kiss.

CONSTANCE   Okay.
        [JULIET *goes to exit*]
        Hey, wait up!

JULIET   I dare not risk discovery in thy company; we must go severally. Dost thou espy yon boneyard?

CONSTANCE   Yes, I see it.

JULIET   My balcony lies three courtyards to the east of that unhallowed ground.

CONSTANCE   Why is it unhallowed?

JULIET   For that the bones of actors, whores and pedants lie there buried and condemned.
        [JULIET *blows a kiss and exits*]

CONSTANCE   Thanks.
        [*Exit* CONSTANCE. *Enter* ROMEO, *furtive, in Juliet's clothing*]

ROMEO   [*aside*] I dare not take the front gate for my leave;
        my father must not see my woman's weeds.
        [*Exit. Softly, from off.*] Constantine ... it is I, Romiet ...

Act III, Scene vi. ❧

The Boneyard.
A distant bell tolls midnight. A watchman cries from off,
'Twelve O'clock and all is well.' Enter CONSTANCE, *scared.*
Creepy night sounds: crows, distant cries ...

CONSTANCE [*singing tunelessly to herself to allay her fear*] I never saw a
Ghost in my life, Ghost in my life, Ghost in my life; I
never saw a Ghost in my life, 'cause there's no such thing.
I never saw a –
[*Suddenly, ghost sounds: wind, chains, smoke. A skeleton-
faced* GHOST *emerges through a trap door. He wears
Constance's red toque with the pom-pom.* CONSTANCE
turns and sees him, and is terrified]
Holy Mary, Mother of God! –

GHOST   A man told me he hadn't had a bite
in three days, so I bit him. I awoke
today and shot an elephant in my
pajamas. How he got there, I know not.
I just flew in from Padua, and zounds,
are my arms tired!

CONSTANCE Who are you?

GHOST Who are you-ou-ou?

CONSTANCE Where'd you get that hat?

GHOST A fo-o-ol's cap.

CONSTANCE Is this some kind of joke?

GHOST My stock in trade.

CONSTANCE A ghostly fool? A jester from the grave?
Are you –? You couldn't be. What play is this?
Could you be ... Yorick?!

GHOST   Na-a-ay. You're it.

CONSTANCE You're it?

GHOST Alas poor fool, you know me well.

CONSTANCE   I do?
Don't speak in riddles, tell me what you mean.

GHOST I mean you script a woman, and a fool
it's not a man you seek, the Manuscript ...

CONSTANCE Do you know something of the Manuscript?!
Do you know who the Author is?

GHOST   A lass.

CONSTANCE	I know, 'alas, alas poor Yorick', so?!
	Who wrote this thing?
GHOST	A beardless bard.
CONSTANCE	A boy?
GHOST	A lass!
CONSTANCE	Oh here we go again, 'alas'!
	Who is the Author?
GHOST	A Fool, a Fool.
CONSTANCE	The Fool and the Author are one in the same?
GHOST	Ha, ha, ha, ha.
CONSTANCE	What's his name?!
GHOST	*Do not forget. This visitation*
	is but to whet thy almost blunted purpose.
	Beware of Tybalt.
	He hath not a sense of humour.
	Audieu, audieu, adieu. Remember me-e-e.
	[GHOST *begins to sink back down the trap*]
CONSTANCE	No, wait! Don't go yet! Yorick!
GHOST	Yo-o-u-u're it.
	[*Exit* GHOST. *Enter* TYBALT]
TYBALT	Hermaphrodite!
CONSTANCE	Who, me? Oh, hi Tybalt.
TYBALT	Greek boy! *The love I bear thee can afford*
	no better term than this: thou art a villain.
CONSTANCE	There must be some mistake. *Therefore farewell.*
	[CONSTANCE *tries to exit*]
TYBALT	*Boy, this shall not excuse the injuries*
	that thou hast done me; therefore turn and draw.
CONSTANCE	No please! I haven't done anything!
TYBALT	*I am for you!*
	[*He draws. Something like an anchovy hangs off the end of*
	his sword. CONSTANCE *recognizes it, and plucks it off*]
CONSTANCE	Good heavens, this is somebody's appendix …

[*mouthing the word*] mine! No. No, please don't hurt me, please!

TYBALT   A l'arme!

[TYBALT *tosses her a sword. She catches it*]

CONSTANCE   Alright, then, come on! [*swishes her sword*] I trained in Cyprus you know, come on. [*swish*] Hit me. [*thumping her chest*] Hit me right here.

[TYBALT *lunges.* CONSTANCE *yelps with fear and fends him off clumsily. Enter* ROMEO *in women's clothing*]

ROMEO   *Hold Tybalt! Good* Constantine! *Put up your swords!*

[ROMEO *comes between the combatants, raising his arms to stop them as in 'Romeo and Juliet'; but here,* TYBALT*'s sword, rather than skewering* CONSTANCE *under* ROMEO*'s arm, gets caught in the flowing fabric of* ROMEO*'s dress.* CONSTANCE *escapes as the two men struggle.* ROMEO *runs off.* TYBALT *looks about, swishes his sword, then runs off after* CONSTANCE]

Act III, Scene vii. ❧

Juliet's balcony and bedchamber.
JULIET, *still in Romeo's clothing, waits for* CONSTANCE.

JULIET   Ay me.

CONSTANCE   [*from off below*] Juliet! Help!

[JULIET *takes a rope ladder from under the bed and throws it down.* CONSTANCE *struggles up and onto the balcony, still bearing the sword*]

JULIET   Catch, love!

CONSTANCE   Tell me the name!

JULIET   Give me my kiss!

[CONSTANCE *gives* JULIET *a chaste peck on the cheek*]
Where's passion in thy curiosity?

CONSTANCE	My life's at stake.
JULIET	My heart's on fire.

[*Pause.* CONSTANCE *works up her nerve and kisses* JULIET *on the mouth.* JULIET *takes over.* CONSTANCE *breaks it off*]

CONSTANCE	Ahem. Now who's the Author?
JULIET	I did lie.
CONSTANCE	You little brat!

[JULIET *picks up* CONSTANCE*'s sword, thrusts it into* CONSTANCE*'s hands, and bares the upper portion of her own left breast*]

JULIET   Now wreak atonement here!
Spear the lie e'en to its bubbling source!

[JULIET *grabs the tip of* CONSTANCE*'s sword and tries to plunge it into her heart.* CONSTANCE *resists*]

CONSTANCE Hang on! There's no need to over-react!

[CONSTANCE *manages to wrest the sword from* JULIET *and tosses it over the balcony*]

JULIET   And I cannot rejoice upon thy sword,
                 I'll die upon my dagger, so!

[JULIET *takes a dagger and winds up to stab herself.* CONSTANCE *intervenes*]

CONSTANCE   No!

[CONSTANCE *wrests the dagger from* JULIET, *flings it over the balcony, and pins* JULIET *down*]

Now listen here. There's something you don't know.
For safety did I first secrete my sex.
I mean! – I'll have to trust you with the truth.
My name is Constance. I'm a woman.

JULIET	Oh.
CONSTANCE	That's right. So that's that.
JULIET	And art thou of Cyprus?
CONSTANCE	Not originally.
JULIET	Then art thou of Lesbos?!

CONSTANCE	What?! I've never been there in my life.
JULIET	O most forbidden love of all!
CONSTANCE	Oh no.
JULIET	Unsanctified desire, more tragic far
	than any star-crossed love 'twixt boy and girl!
CONSTANCE	Now wait.
JULIET	Once more am I a virgin maid.
	O take me to thine island's curv'ed shore,
	and lay me on the bosom of the sand;
	there sing to me the psalm that Sappho wrote;
	her hymn to love will be our Song of Songs.
CONSTANCE	I'm not up on Sappho.
JULIET	Then we'll compose an epic of our own.
CONSTANCE	But I'm not – you know – I'm not … a lesbian. At all.
	That's just a rumour. I've never been involved with a
	woman.
	Unless you count that one time in grade eight
	when Ginnie Radclyffe did my portrait.
	Her mother worked, and Ginnie was a cubist.
	She said she had to have a detailed tour
	of my physique for authenticity.
	Ginnie had such poignant hands and wrists.
	But I never painted her.
JULIET	She died.
CONSTANCE	She's married now and can't recall a thing.
JULIET	A portrait hangs unfinished in thy heart.
CONSTANCE	I know I felt bereft. But that was then.
JULIET	Make ready now to paint me in her stead.
	So mix and frame the colours on this bed.
CONSTANCE	I don't know how.
JULIET	Be thou the mirror pool of my desire:
	reflect my love as thou dost ape my form.
CONSTANCE	Thou wouldst distort the pool, thy looking glass,
	with words of love like careless pebbles tossed;

the rippling waters tell a loving lie,
and show my face to thee as 't'were thine own.
Still waters would reflect an ag'ed crone.

JULIET   More beauty in thy testament of years,
than in the face of smooth and depthless youth.
Nay, lovelier by far, now that I see
the sculpting hand of time upon thy brow;
O look on me with eyes that looked on life
before I e'er was born an infant blind.
O touch me with those hands that held thy quill
before I learned to read and write my name.
And thus with every look and touch, entwine
my poor young thread into thy richer weave.

CONSTANCE   Okay.

JULIET   Tomorrow will they find one corpse entwined,
when, having loved each other perfectly,
our deaths proclaim one night, eternity.

CONSTANCE   Eternity …

JULIET   I have a vial of poison hidden here; [*concealed in her shirt*]
it will dispatch us with the morning lark.

CONSTANCE   But for now, the nightingale doth sing.

[JULIET *leans down and* CONSTANCE *reaches into her shirt*]

What have we here?

[CONSTANCE *withdraws her hand from* JULIET *'s shirt, holding a Manuscript Page*]

Oh shit.

[*She unrolls the scroll and reads:*]

    'Thy demons rest not till they've eaten thee.
    Get Desdemon and merge this trinity,
    or never live to see another Birthdy.'

I forgot. It's my birthday today.

[*The warp effects begin.* JULIET *is terrified*]

JULIET   Constance!

CONSTANCE   Hang on, Julie-e-et!

[*The warp ends, to reveal* JULIET *and* CONSTANCE, *huddled together, eyes closed, still on Juliet's bed. Nothing, apparently, has changed*]

It's alright.

[*They release one another and scan the room*]

False alarm.

[*They chuckle and lie back again as* JULIET *begins to re-arrange the pillows on the bed. Suddenly she screams –*]

JULIET   Ah-h-h-h-h-h-h-h-!!!

[*– and leaps back to reveal* DESDEMONA, *who rises: a Phoenix from the pillows*]

DESDEMONA   'Tis strange, i'faith. 'Tis passing wondrous strange.

CONSTANCE   Desdemona.

DESDEMONA   *O perjured pedant, thou dost stone my heart.*

CONSTANCE   [*about to introduce* JULIET] Desdemona, this is –

[DESDEMONA *takes up a pillow*]

DESDEMONA   *Put out the light, and then put out the light.*

[DESDEMONA *brings the pillow down on* CONSTANCE'*s head*]

CONSTANCE   No! Help!!! [*muffled etc. …*]

JULIET   Hold!

DESDEMONA   Thy fool's cap is a Turkish document,
           and thou, base strumpet, hast seduced my lord!

[DESDEMONA *raises the pillow*]

CONSTANCE   No! No way, I swear!

[*The pillow comes down again.* JULIET *grabs another pillow and offers it to* DESDEMONA]

JULIET   Kill me in her stead!

[DESDEMONA *ignores* JULIET]

DESDEMONA   I saw thee fingering his very jewels!
           A diamond necklace that would ransom kings!

[*Pillow up*]

CONSTANCE Oh that!

DESDEMONA *Down strumpet!*

[JULIET *hits* DESDEMONA *with the pillow, but* DESDEMONA *disarms her easily and knocks her flying*]

CONSTANCE *Kill me tomorrow!*

DESDEMONA *It is too late!*

[*Pillow down*]

JULIET [*exiting*] Help! Murther!

[CONSTANCE, *her head still beneath the pillow, reaches under her shirt, yanks off the diamond necklace, and holds its broad golden clasp before* DESDEMONA'*s eyes*]

DESDEMONA Ah ha! [*reading inscription*] 'For gentle Desdemona, upon thy birthday, love Othello.'

[CONSTANCE'*s hands drop to the bed and go limp*]

[*smiling*] Oh. It is my birthday today. I had forgot. [*to* CONSTANCE] I'm sorry. [*suddenly remembering*] Constance! [*whips the pillow up*]

   Not dead? Not yet quite dead?

[*A beat, then* CONSTANCE *takes a huge gasp of air*]

CONSTANCE Happy Birthday.

[CONSTANCE *takes the pillow from* DESDEMONA *and whacks her with it, knocking her down*]

TYBALT [*off*] Greek boy!

CONSTANCE Oh no, it's Tybalt. Pretend I'm dead, and tell Juliet to meet us at the Crypt.

[CONSTANCE *lies back on the bed*]

DESDEMONA Who?

TYBALT [*off*] The worms line up to feast on thee!

CONSTANCE Juliet! The lady of the house, she was here a second ago.

DESDEMONA I saw no-one, save a spindly boy.

[TYBALT *enters over the balcony, sword drawn.* CONSTANCE *plays dead*]

TYBALT Ha!

DESDEMONA [*pointing to* CONSTANCE] Dead! Quite dead!

TYBALT   Well killed! I'll drag him to the charnel house.

DESDEMONA   Sir, how might I know Juliet?

TYBALT   She is a young and lovely sylph in flowing rose-hued silk.

[*Exit* DESDEMONA. JULIET *appears at the balcony in time to see* TYBALT *dragging* CONSTANCE *off*]

JULIET   [*aside*] Constance dead? *Is it e'en so?*

[*Exit* TYBALT *with* CONSTANCE. JULIET *raises her dagger aloft*]

Then I defy you stars! Constance, *I will lie with thee tonight.*

[*Exit* JULIET]

Act III, Scene viii. ❧

Beneath Constance's balcony.
Enter ROMEO, *still in Juliet's clothing, with rope ladder.*
Enter DESDEMONA. *She watches* ROMEO *toss one end of the rope ladder over a balustrade above, in an attempt to scale the wall to the balcony.*

DESDEMONA   [*aside*] By Tybalt's own account, must this be Juliet.
Here is the rose-hued silk ...
but nowhere do I see the lovely sylph.
[*to* ROMEO] What ho, I have a message for you,
Lady.

[ROMEO *sees* DESDEMONA]

ROMEO   [*aside*] *O, she doth teach the torches to burn bright!*

DESDEMONA   Constance doth await us at the Crypt, ma'am.

ROMEO   I am no ma'am, but man, and worship thee.

DESDEMONA   We'd make short work of thee in Cyprus, lad.

Act III, Scene ix. ❧

A Crypt and the Boneyard surrounding it.
The crypt is eerily lit, and the boneyard that surrounds it is
darker, à la silhouette. TYBALT *arranges* CONSTANCE
upon a raised slab in the crypt.

TYBALT   Lie thou there, inverted nature.
      [*He starts to exit, pauses, then turns back*]
      If curiosity doth stay my leave,
      it's of an wholesome scientific kind –
      to take the measure of his member.
      [DESDEMONA, *followed by* ROMEO, *enters the graveyard*
      as TYBALT *goes to remove* CONSTANCE*'s longjohns*]

ROMEO   [*lying on a tombstone*] Come lie with me upon this
      marble bed.
      [ROMEO*'s voice startles* TYBALT *away from* CONSTANCE]

TYBALT   I'd not be caught, mine hands upon his hose,
      and of his self-same cloth thought to be cut.
      [*Exit* TYBALT *into the graveyard, as* DESDEMONA *con-*
      tinues to search for the correct crypt. CONSTANCE *sits up*]

DESDEMONA   'Blessed be the man that spares these stones. And cursed
      be he that moves my bones: William –
      [TYBALT *sees* ROMEO *through the gloom and approaches*]

TYBALT   What maiden corse lies fest'ring here for crows to
      peck?
      [ROMEO *reaches up and pulls* TYBALT *toward him*]
      Ha-ha! No corse but fresh, and laid out for the
      pecking.
      [TYBALT *picks* ROMEO *up and carries him off, ardently.*
      CONSTANCE *resumes her death pose in response to the*
      sound of someone entering. It is JULIET. *She approaches*
      CONSTANCE *and raises her dagger, poised to slay herself*]

JULIET   *O happy dagger!*

This is thy sheath; there rust, and let me die.
[JULIET *starts her fatal upswing, but before she can stab herself*]

CONSTANCE Juliet?

[JULIET *screams*]

JULIET *Not dead?*

[CONSTANCE *shakes her head*]

Not yet quite dead?

CONSTANCE   Not one bit dead.

JULIET [*seizing and kissing* CONSTANCE*'s hand*]

O Love! O resurrected Love, O Constance!

[JULIET, *overcome, embraces* CONSTANCE, *her dagger still in hand.* DESDEMONA *dashes into the crypt and draws her sword upon* JULIET]

DESDEMONA   Unhand the damsel, thou rapacious knave!

[JULIET *cowers against* CONSTANCE *as* DESDEMONA *rears back, about to lunge*]

CONSTANCE Hold! Desdemona, this is Juliet, the young lady of the house ... Remember?

DESDEMONA   Zounds! Doth no one in Verona sail straight?

CONSTANCE Juliet, this is Desdemona, an old friend of mine from Cyprus.

JULIET   With friends like this, thou wantest not for foes.

DESDEMONA   Dost thou dare impugn my honour, poppet?

JULIET   Aye, and what if I durst?

DESDEMONA   Then dare to die!

CONSTANCE Wait –

JULIET   That do I dare any day for love!

DESDEMONA Ha.

JULIET   I twice did nearly slay myself today
for love of her whom thou didst seek to kill.

DESDEMONA   *I love her better than thou canst devise,*
for naught I did in hate, but all in honour.

JULIET   Hateful honour!

DESDEMONA   Dishonourable love!

JULIET   'Tis I that Constance loveth best.

DESDEMONA   Pish, come Constance, let's hie home.

CONSTANCE   Home.

JULIET   Constance will not leave my side.

DESDEMONA   She hath naught to live for here.

JULIET   But everything for which to die.

DESDEMONA   In Cyprus hath she that for which to kill.

JULIET   She is a lover, not a warrior;
a votary of Venus, not of Mars.

a person bound by religious vows

DESDEMONA   Nay, she hath proved herself a very Martian:
she nearly killed a man in Cyprus.

JULIET   [*to* CONSTANCE]
No!

CONSTANCE   Well ... yes, but –

JULIET   She nearly died for love with me!

DESDEMONA   [*to* CONSTANCE]
Thou didst?!

CONSTANCE   Sorry.

DESDEMONA   Constance, it be not too late to save
thy reputation, and redeem thyself.

CONSTANCE   Oh no?

DESDEMONA   Return with me to Cyprus; take this sword,
and dip it deep to drink Iago's gorge.

[DESDEMONA *puts the sword into* CONSTANCE*'s hand*]

JULIET   Remain! To one blade, we'll two hearts afix,
then sail together 'cross the River Styx.

[JULIET *puts the dagger into* CONSTANCE*'s other hand*]

DESDEMONA   Nay, come and kill.

JULIET   Nay, stay and die.

DESDEMONA   Nay come!

JULIET   Nay stay!

DESDEMONA   Nay kill!!

JULIET   Nay die!!

CONSTANCE Nay nay!! – Nay. Just ... nay ... both of you. I've had it
with all the tragic tunnel vision around here. You have
no idea what – life is a hell of a lot more complicated than
you think! Life – real life – is a big mess. Thank
goodness. And every answer spawns another question;
and every question blossoms with a hundred different
answers; and if you're lucky you'll always feel somewhat
confused. Life Is –! ... Life is ...
    a harmony of polar opposites,
    with gorgeous mixed-up places in between,
    where inspiration steams up from a rich
    Sargasso stew that's odd and flawed and full
    of gems and worn-out boots and sunken ships –
Desdemona, I thought you were different: I thought you
were my friend, I worshipped you. But you're just like
Othello – gullible and violent. Juliet, if you really loved
me, you wouldn't want me to die. But you were more in
love with death, 'cause death is easier to love. Never
mind. I must have been a monumental fool to think that
I could save you from yourselves ... Fool...

DESDEMONA Nay, thou speakst wise.

JULIET   Aye, fools were never wise.

DESDEMONA Could any fool reveal, how we were wont to err?

JULIET Or get us to concede, what we will gladly swear?

CONSTANCE What's that?

DESDEMONA To live by questions, not by their solution.

JULIET To trade our certainties, for thy confusion.

CONSTANCE Do you really mean that?

    [JULIET *and* DESDEMONA *nod,* 'yes.']

GHOST [*under the stage*] *Swear. Swear.*

DESDEMONA
& JULIET We swear.

CONSTANCE Then I was right about your plays. They were comedies
after all, not tragedies. I was wrong about one thing,

though: I thought only a Wise Fool could turn tragedy to comedy.

GHOST   [*below*] Ha, ha, ha, ha, ha!

CONSTANCE   Yorick.

GHOST   Na-a-ay. You're it.

CONSTANCE   I'm it? ... I'm it. *I'm* the Fool!

GHOST   A lass.

CONSTANCE   A lass!

GHOST   A beardless bard.

CONSTANCE   'The Fool and the Author are one and the same' ...

GHOST   Ha-ha-ha-ha-ha!

CONSTANCE   That's me. I'm the Author!

[*A golden hand rises up through the surface of the slab upon which Constance lay. The hand holds a scrolled Manuscript page.* CONSTANCE *takes the page and unscrolls it*]
It says ...

    'For those who have the eyes to see:

    Take care – for what you see, just might be thee.'

[*She looks at* DESDEMONA *and* JULIET]

    'Where two plus one adds up to one, not three.'

Goodnight Desdemona. Good morning Juliet.

DESDEMONA
& JULIET   Happy Birthday Constance.

[*The warp ensues. It is a choreographed transformation involving all the actors: the Crypt and Boneyard turn back into Constance's office at Queen's. During the transformation, the actors exit and enter with gold-wrapped boxes – birthday presents for* CONSTANCE. *Their costumes transform as well, until each actor wears an odd combination of her or his various costumes.*

When the warp is over, CONSTANCE *is alone in her office at Queen's. Both she and the office are precisely as they were at the onset of the first warp at the end of Act I: the phone receiver dangles by its cord, and* CONSTANCE *is leaning over with just her — hatless — head in the wastebasket. She straightens up and looks about her, a little disoriented. She tentatively touches herself as if to confirm her reality, bringing one hand up to her head. She feels her pen behind her ear, removes it, and looks at it. It has turned to solid gold, feather and all*]

Act III, The Epilogue. ❧

Enter the CHORUS *holding the Ghost's skeleton mask.*

CHORUS   The alchemy of ancient hieroglyphs
has permeated the unconscious mind
of Constance L. and manifested form,
where there was once subconscious dreamy thought.
The best of friends and foes exist within,
where archetypal shadows come to light
and doff their monster masks when we say 'boo'.
Where mingling and unmingling opposites
performs a wondrous feat of alchemy,
and spins grey matter, into precious gold.

[*Lights and Music. The company dances.*]

Ann-Marie MacDonald is a playwright and actor. She has lived for many years in Toronto, but her family roots are in Cape Breton Island. She was conceived in Edmonton, born in West Germany, and grew up all over Ontario before fleeing to Montreal to train at The National Theatre School.

Since graduating in 1980, her double career has ranged widely, but her theatrical roots and the bulk of her work have been in fringe theatre. She has worked collectively and collaboratively in the creation and performance of many new works, among them *This Is for You, Anna* by The Anna Project and *Nancy Prew: Clue in the Fast Lane,* co-written with Beverley Cooper.

Goodnight Desdemona (Good Morning Juliet) is MacDonald's first solo writing work, and has been honoured with a Chalmers Canadian Play Award and the 1990 Governor General's Award for Drama.

Her second play, *The Arab's Mouth*, premiered at Toronto's Factory Theatre in October 1990.

Other drama titles available from
COACH HOUSE PRESS

Lilies: Or The Revival of a Romantic Drama
MICHEL MARC BOUCHARD
"The most powerful play to emerge from Quebec in many years. Its language, inspired by preraphaelite paintings, is full of the plumage of youthful beauty and of exalted emotions that can never quite have existed. Bouchard's script lives up to its magnificent effrontery."
— Ray Conlogue, *The Globe and Mail*

Quebec Voices
NORMAND CHAURETTE, RENE GINGRAS,
RENE DANIEL DUBOIS
"A valuable and timely publication in giving anglophone readers access, in English translation, to some of the most interesting plays in recent Quebec theatre."
— S.I. Lockerbie, *British Journal of Canadian Studies*

Quiet in the Land
ANNE CHISLETT
Winner of the 1983 Governor General's Award for Drama, *Quiet in the Land* centres on a small Amish community near Elora, Ontario, committed to non-violence and simple religious life. "Written with exemplary compassion and understanding, the play has genuine texture." — Jamie Portman

Other drama titles available from
COACH HOUSE PRESS

The Book of Jessica
LINDA GRIFFITHS AND MARIA CAMPBELL
"A fascinating study not only of the tortuous birth of a magnificent play but of the relationship of two women driven apart and bound together by a maelstrom of internal and external forces."
— Janet Silman, *The Globe and Mail*

Willful Acts
MARGARET HOLLINGSWORTH
"Women and their relationships, both with each other and with men, is the topic of the five Hollingsworth plays gathered in *Willful Acts*. They are all tantalizing pieces of theatre." — *Now Magazine*

The Farm Show
TED JOHNS
The prototype of the Canadian documentary play, this Theatre Passe Muraille collective work offers a generous, humanistic portrait of life in a farming community in Clinton County, Ontario. Its enduring messages of hope and hardship have made this book a contemporary classic.

Farther West / New World
JOHN MURRELL
Winner of the Floyd S. Chalmers and Canadian Authors Association Best Play awards. "Murrell's dramatic landscape ... emphasizes women as creators of their own rules and environments."
— Martin Knelman, *Saturday Night*

The End / A Day at the Beach
JOHN PALMER
The End: "A fiendishly organized, accelerating farce, worked out with brilliant dexterity." — Urjo Kareda, *The Globe and Mail* • A Day at the Beach: "The most capable and deeply expressed treatment of gay themes I've seen for a long, long time." — Dayne Ogilvie, *Extra!*

The Other Side of the Dark
JUDITH THOMPSON
Winner of the 1989 Governor-General's Award for Drama, this volume includes Thompson's most-acclaimed play, *The Crackwalker*, as well as *I Am Yours*, *Pink*, and *Tornado*. "Thompson is a powerful and original voice in Canadian theatre." — Robert Crew, *The Toronto Star*

Bag Babies: A Comedy of (Bad) Manners
ALLAN STRATTON
"A brilliant, funny satire about urban hunger and homelessness, about the parvenu rich, about the wretched pomposity of the news media and 'greed without guilt.' [This is] theatre very much at the centre of life."— Michael Valpy, *The Globe and Mail*

Words in Play: Three Comedies
ALLAN STRATTON
"Stratton's genius is in taking everyday situations and — like Molière — giving them the right kind of comic or bizarre twist to make us notice the real issue driving the plot: the struggle between good and evil or illusion and reality, and the foibles of human beings revealed in the struggle to cope." — *Literature and Language*

Other drama titles available from
COACH HOUSE PRESS

The Work: Conversations with English Canadian Playwrights
ROBERT WALLACE AND CYNTHIA ZIMMERMAN, EDS.
Interviews with Hrant Alianak, Carol Bolt, Tom Cone, Michael Cook, Rex Deverell, David Fennario, Larry Fineberg, David French, Ken Gass, John Gray, Herschel Hardin, Tom Hendry, Margaret Hollingsworth, Michael Hollingsworth, Martin Kinch, Ken Mitchell, John Palmer, Sharon Pollock, Erika Ritter, Sheldon Rosen, Lawrence Russell, Rick Salutin, Paul Thompson, Bryan Wade, George F. Walker, and Tom Walmsley.

Love and Anger
GEORGE F. WALKER
Winner of a Chalmers Canadian Play award. "Walker's writing is tauter and tougher than ever. *Love And Anger* is a triumph, a fiercely comic flowering of a major and mature talent."
— Doug Bale, *London Free Press*

Nothing Sacred
GEORGE F. WALKER
Winner of the 1988 Governor General's Award for Drama. "Russian writer Ivan Turgenev first popularized the term 'nihilist' in his great 1862 novel *Fathers and Sons*, one of the most vivid creations of Russian literature. In *Nothing Sacred*, Walker has caught the novel's broad sympathies and subtle play of ideas in a brilliant stage version. Although he amplifies the gentle humour of Turgenev's tragicomedy to near-farcical levels, the result is spell-binding."
— John Bemrose, *Maclean's*

Other drama titles available from
COACH HOUSE PRESS

The Power Plays
GEORGE F. WALKER
Investigator T.M. Power and his sidekick do battle with the corrupt
and capricious, decadent and desperate, rich and famous, and makers
and breakers of culture and control in this trilogy of comic thriller
plays, *Gossip*, *Filthy Rich* and *The Art of War*.

Three Plays
GEORGE F. WALKER
Walker's unerring eye for detail and his ability to combine these details
into a world at once mysterious and comedic are brilliantly displayed
in *Bagdad Saloon*, *Beyond Mozambique* and *Ramona and the White
Slaves*.

Editor for the Press: Robert Wallace
Cover Illustration: Sue Le Page (Costume design for
GHOST, *Goodnight Desdemona, 1990* production)
Author photograph: Cheryl Daniels
Text design: Nelson Adams

COACH HOUSE PRESS
401 (rear) Huron Street
Toronto, Canada M5S 2G5